AF567011

Appalachia Under Thirty

Volume 19

2016

Volume 19

Appalachia Under Thirty

Co-Editors: Pauletta Hansel (Managing Editor),
Michael Henson and Sherry Cook Stanforth
Layout & Design: Elizabeth H. Murphy - Illusion Studios
Intern: Bridget Reilly (Xavier University)

Founding Editor: Jim Webb
Founding Publisher: Robb Webb

PMS&G logo courtesy of Colleen Anderson of *Mother Wit*

Cover: "Sunday Afternoon" by Angelyn DeBord

Typset in Adobe Garamond Pro & Artbrush
ISBN 978-1-939929-63-1
Library of Congress Control Number: 2016951761

Published in cooperation with Dos Madres Press

www.dosmadres.com

Dos Madres Press, Inc. is an Ohio Not For Profit Corporation and a 501 (c) (3) qualified public charity. Contributions are tax deductible.

PINE MOUNTAIN SAND & GRAVEL CO.
Whitesburg, Kentucky

NAME ____________________________________

For Period Ending ____________________, 195___

Earnings	No. Of	Rate	Amount	
Tons @				
Hours @				
Hours @				
	Total Earnings			

DEDUCTIONS	AMOUNT	
Cash		
W'holding Tax		
S. S. Tax		
Fuel		
U. M. W. of A.		
Supplies		
Transfers		

Total Deductions		
AMOUNT DUE		
Overdraft		
TOTAL DUE EMPLOYEE		
Amount Due Company		

Received of Pine Mountain Sand & Gravel Co.. amount shown above in full payment for wages.

Signed: ____________________________________

This Check Includes Your
Vacation Pay Bonus.

*"Don't worry about the mule going blind,
just load the wagon"*

TABLE OF CONTENTS

ABOUT THE SOUTHERN APPALACHIAN WRITERS COOPERATIVE

In 1974, a group of writers and activists gathered at Highlander Center in New Market, Tennessee, to form what became the Southern Appalachian Writers Cooperative. From its very beginning, SAWC was intended to support writers in our efforts to take control of our regional identity and to take action, individually and collectively, on the issues that impact our land and our people.

For over four decades, the Southern Appalachian Writers Cooperative has provided a place for us to come together to share our work and our struggles, and to ponder how these things affect, not only our work, but also our relationships to each other, to the region and to the broader culture. During the 1970s, SAWC sponsored readings and published *New Ground*, an anthology of contemporary Appalachian literature. In the 1980s, the Appalachian Poetry Project, initiated by Gurney Norman with poets George Ella Lyon and Bob Henry Baber, brought new life into SAWC. Poets and writers from throughout the Appalachian region gathered in their own and one another's communities and celebrated together at Highlander Center. SAWC has met (almost) annually since this time, usually at Highlander Research and Education Center and always in the fall. Through this and other SAWC Writers Gathering and by sponsoring local readings and the literary magazine, *Pine Mountain Sand & Gravel*, the Southern Appalachian Writers Cooperative continues its original mission to foster community and activism among and encourage publication of Appalachia's writers.

Pine Mountain Sand & Gravel was founded in the mid-1980s by brothers Jim and Robb Webb. Their company, Appalapple Productions (Jim being a resident of Letcher County, Kentucky, and Robb of the Big Apple) produced three volumes of the journal before passing the torch to the Southern Appalachian Writers Cooperative in 1996. In its thirty some years of publication, *PMS&G* has produced 19 volumes of contemporary Appalachian writing, and been stewarded by 13 editors and co-editors. In 2015, the Southern Appalachian Writers Cooperative in collaboration with Dos Madres Press published *Quarried: Three Decades of Pine Mountain Sand & Gravel. Quarried,* edited by editor emeritus Richard Hague, collects early writing by notable Appalachian authors including Lee Howard, George Ella Lyon, Jeff Daniel Marion, Jim Wayne Miller and Gurney Norman alongside newer work by many of Appalachia's current established and emerging poets, essayists and novelists.

Pine Mountain Sand & Gravel is now an annual, themed journal. The current call for submissions, purchase information, a list of upcoming readings, and information about the Southern Appalachian Writers Cooperative's fall and other gatherings can always be found at *sawconline.net.* You may also contact *Pine Mountain Sand & Gravel* at: pmsg.journal@gmail.com.

INTRODUCTION
Pine Mountain Sand & Gravel Volume 19
Appalachia Under Thirty

For this issue of *Pine Mountain Sand & Gravel*, we invited writers under thirty to talk about their lives and issues. And, not to exclude older writers, we invited those over thirty to reflect on their under-thirty experiences. We wanted to open the door to new writers and to keep the older writers within the fold. We received a wealth of material from each. These poems, stories, essays, and memoirs are, by turns, angry, pensive, joyful—reflective, we think, of the exciting work being done in this second generation of the Appalachian literary renaissance. We hope you enjoy reading this issue as much as we have enjoyed putting it together.

The editors, *Pine Mountain Sand & Gravel*
Pauletta Hansel
Michael Henson
Sherry Cook Stanforth

Melissa Helton

Appalachian Pastoral

Mountains swell like stopped green
ocean, like the bicep resting
at a valley of elbow. Take a bird's path
— the red tail hawk that fans to perch
on pine; darting eyes outline a boy

verging on manhood like the last day
winter holds back the river. That boy
leans in the shadow and cushion
of poplar, watching the forest—
the gray squirrel inching to inspect him

tail a nervous twitch, and the copperhead
coiling under the striated cliff
edge, quiet in the dark.
They are wary as he watches them.
Hours he sits. The hawk, he will kill

one day, once spring has released
the river. And he will carry one
tail feather—always
to remember those years, sitting
on creekrock the size of shoulderblades,

cold runoff sliding over him—unable
to tell shale from skin. He catches silverfish,
lets them slip through his fingers,
and on the banks around him
open the lone white flowers of bloodroot.

Cathy Cultice Lentes

The Fox

Mother drove us home from the city at dusk,
our green Pontiac a solid steamer skimming
over snowy waves, my mind still rehearsing
a small calamity of scales, slim fingers failing
those 88 cold keys though weekly we went
to the house near the college, and I was dropped
like a late autumn leaf, spun across the yard, up
the wooden stairs to the teacher's door where I
knocked so gently I hoped never to be heard.
Music rose for me in poetry's leaping lines, the
whisper of story pages turning, but mother
played, so I must serve my bench sentence.

That winter eve as we curved toward home
and the tall cases covered with friendly books, my
small heart tried to be thankful as a girl given
piano lessons should be, but I was failing at that too,
and then in the misting twilight, a red fox sizzled
like a promise across the field making for those tall
staccato eighth notes of the woods, and only I
heard her fur's hum, felt her heart pulse, saw the
sure padded story she was making. She was not afraid.
And despite the cold and lonely night, she knew,
and I knew then, exactly where we belonged,
the only trail to follow.

Kelsey A. Solomon

My first cup of coffee

was in a plastic yellow cup with a withered handle
while I sat in Mamaw's kitchen, a gathering place for
every Easter, every Thanksgiving, and every Christmas,
but a getaway for me on Saturday nights before
church in the morning. After a certain age
she stopped talking to me about Jesus, because
she thought I knew him, whatever that meant.
I still don't know. She told me stories about the
neighbors, churchfolk, the coyotes, the normal
gossip, and when she paused to sip her coffee, I asked
her why she drank it. She slid her cup to me and said,
"Try it for yourself," and when I did, I burnt my lips.
Brimstone, I thought, with a hint of dirt, but after a
moment, the taste set in. I asked for more with a
little sugar, and she said, "You'll learn to drink it black."

Nancy Dillingham

Gnat Smoke

When they swarmed
in great waves
on warm summer nights

we stuffed damp rags
and a handful of shavings
into tin cans and lit them

sat with family and neighbors
in the chip yard
until drowsy

then found our way
to the house
where we washed bare feet

dirty hands and faces
in the kitchen sink
before stumbling to bed

the music of jar flies
and laughter drifting
through open windows

seeping like smoke
into sleep
and dreams

Shawna Kay Rodenberg

The Stray

In the dust around a trailer's front step, Jeanie and I
messed with a cat, sick and snotty from a wolf worm
anchored in its neck. She ran to the neighbor's for tweezers
while I tried with my fingernails to pull out the worm.
The cat howled. The worm snapped back into its hole.
I stretched wide the opening, strained to see inside.
The worm coiled gray inside slick pink and thin veins.
We chided the cat for hunting baby rabbits, for sticking
its cruel head into furry burrows where wolf worms wait.
I tried with the tweezers. No luck— the same snapping back,
the same howling, till Jeanie's mamaw yelled out the kitchen window
for us to leave the worm be. A larva, *larvy*, she said,
it would flourish and fly away soon enough. The cat
was a daft and willing vessel for change. She was right.

Dory L. Hudspeth

What Comes Back

The boys throwing rocks
were testing the air, their aim,
and their father's advice,
as they lobbed stone after stone
at the hornet nest. Brothers
and cousins lined up taking turns
with their chosen stone,
but ready to run.
The nest was high
enough in the sycamore tree
in the back pasture to be a challenge.
They wanted to believe,
and to not believe,
that hornets can follow
the path of a stone back
to the thrower, as surely
as a son will remember
his father's warning.

Connie Jordan Green

Looking Back

My youth? I hear it mostly in…
Larry Levis

the shrill whistle
of my father's cupped hands

calling my sisters and me from play,
summoning us from the vacant lot
behind the government's cemesto

houses, hear it in the summer rain
on our porch roof where we swapped
comics with neighborhood children,

hear it in my mother's song, steam
frizzing her hair while she ironed
ruffle, pleat, and tucks of our cotton

dresses, know my youth in the scent
of corn tasseling in a backyard garden,
dust of chalkboard, sweat of gym clothes,

pungent chlorine of summer swims,
touch the years of youth in sun-dried
sheets and paste-waxed floors, a life

that flowed with the years,
seamless as a stream wearing
away rock, carving its bed.

Misty Skaggs

Sugar

On a hilltop faraway, in another time, I had a pony. Papaw tethered her to one of the tall, thin maple trees situated in the dead center of the green acre of clover we called the front yard. And I stood, hypnotized at the picture window, pressing the chubby flesh of my cheeks against the warm plexi-glass. I watched her lope lazily in wide, steady circles stopping to snap up mouths full of sweet, tender grass. Her long pink tongue tickled me and when she'd stomp her feet and throw up dust, I'd stomp mine, too. Mommy said I was too young for a pony, and at four years old, I was. But she was a gift horse, an unplanned present from the absent father to his bastard daughter. The only thing he'd ever brought me before was a Cabbage Patch Kid without her adoption papers and half of a Reese's peanut butter cup.

My young busty, bumpkin of a mother couldn't quite bring herself to refuse when Frankie brought his beat-up, pick-up down our long driveway with a sparkle in those blue eyes of his, eyes wide and clear and so like mine. She had a big heart and he had a palomino pony prancing around the bed of his truck, tethered to a tool box. The loose ends of a big, pink bow tied in a sloppy knot around its neck got trampled and tangled in the shit around its feet. A shock of shiny mane fell across her forehead and the chocolate brown splashes of color in her tan coat caught the spring time sunshine. And I called her Sugar.

"Now, sweetie, sugar…" Frankie began when he stepped down out of the dusty, black Ford.

I had never called him Daddy. Still don't.

His snake skin boots crunched gravel as he strode toward the two of us with purpose, grinning to reveal a row of small, white, perfectly fake teeth. The stiff collar of his plaid, Western shirt was open wide across his chest and a thin, gold crucifix glinted through the bramble of hair there. Absentmindedly reaching up, with a thick thumb and index finger, he smoothed down his full mustache. It was like a blond Burt Reynolds had swept down all the way from Hollywood, into the hills and out to the Ridge, especially to visit us. We were both blushing.

Mommy was harder than her curves would lead you to believe. She put her hands on her soft hips and shot him one of her squint-eyed, scathing looks. The kind of look that makes you feel guilty and you're not even sure why.

"I know what you're thinking, sweetheart," he continued. "But you worry too much! I broke that pony myself, just for my baby girl!"

I seem to remember the pitch of his voice being a little high. But somehow still thick and rich and dripping honey. I definitely remember he was a smooth operator. Confidently sliding one arm around my itty bitty body and the other around my mother's waist, he lifted me up to run my baby fingers over Sugar's coat. I buried the other little girl hand in the golden curls at the nape of his neck. When he smiled, we wanted to trust him.

Joshua Jones

The Dog

"I am sleeping in the bed I never liked
and Junior that dog
is with me made my nose run and itch,
and I felt
down beside me, in a haze
and, for a brief moment, like I'd choke.

I thought
it was your "Dumb animal, ugly as my
daddy's hairy arm."

Jeremy Paden

the angel of the chicken coop

is so much like an eight-year-old girl
who clucks & fusses over her flock
of Araucana & Australorps
of Pearl Leghorns & Chanteclers

who scatters seed & feed
& chases cats away in fits
of rage that turn to laughter

who collects worms & grubs
from two fields over to feed
her favorite rooster, a crested
cream & caramel colored cock

that struts about the yard like
some demigod, some professor
of rhetoric & philosophy

expounding on the metaphysics
of barnyard dignity until she
scoops him up in her arms
& dresses him in scarves & hats

Aubrey Stanforth

Bedtime Story

The Dipper scoops out indigo
and dumps it back
into light
            gas
                        time
                                    space
a world unknown

Shooting stars
stardust
dusty rocks
rock dust
dusted sugar crystals
glued to a blue surface

We watch in astrighast:
Orion turns to shoot
Venus, planted on
Cassiopeia's finger, yet
Virgo shall steal
shatter
and throw
letting glimmer trickle down
then rest
in the worn sky

Linda Parsons

Homing

In the day's gloaming, granddaughters raid
the honeysuckle, plunder lilies and lacecap
hydrangea, their blooming path an emergent
fairy ring. Only in the grimmest of tales
would I squash their parade on my new-mown
lawn, bits silvery as pebbles in Hansel's pockets.
The breadcrumbs come later, burdened with rescue
in the deep-dark wood—famine upon the land,
a poor woodcutter, a stepmother happy to strand
children among beasts. I have strewn this story
like grain and the reap of its crushing, like all omens
longed for in the dearth of childhood. I have dropped
my crusts step by step, lived until hope shone on all
that in any other forest would be lost—the fire
never dying through hungried night, the gumdrop
doors eaten and eaten, no bones but in hard telling,
the moon's white bird leading all the way
back to the good father's house.

Roberta Schultz

Perspective

The Italian man in coveralls paints a mural
of Wiedemann's Fine Beer on Volz's Market.
He leans three stories up on nothing but
a ladder, blue rag bulging from back pocket.

I watched his progress after school from 12th
and Columbia. Monday, just the base
of goblet beaded with sweat. Friday's rise—
Bohemian lager cresting to foam head.

How can it look so real this far away
when the painter stands only bubbles tall?
His beer glass towers almost three flights high.
White swell drizzles over the thin glass rim.

Fresh golden whorls smoothed over crumbling brick.
This *Starry Night*, a sky for thirsty work.

Chuck Stringer

Reaching the New World

for Vic

At the point where these two rivers meet
summer called to us: first the Clinch's dark

water getting deeper and deeper as we
waded naked into the channel; then the slow

Tennessee current pulling us past
the water snakes we couldn't see, couldn't

hear, but knew to be winding there;
the silent porch lights of houses crowded

on the opposite shore, and their light
that skipped like stones; the quiet splashes

of our strokes back to our camp. Inside
the tent, we lay on our sleeping bags

and talked about sex, the White Album, thrills
of our Freshman year, and all the girls

we wanted to date that fall in high school.
Finally the hour, the constant buzz

of cicadas, the fire's smoldering red glow
lulled us to sleep. Later, awakened

by the engine of a passing barge, we watched
the beam of a searchlight as it swept

from shore to shore on its way downriver.
And, sometime in the night, didn't the wind

howl and blow as we dreamed of what stirred
in that ancient mound we had pitched

the tent next to? We didn't wake until noon
when we felt the sun's heat filtering

through hickories, oaks, and pines. Fresh
as the Clinch and Tennessee air,

we raced to the end of the point and dove
into clear water, rising in a world

known only to the two of us, on a day
now all our own.

Hilda Downer

Looking up from inside a jar, the stars are holes

I wanted to call mama
when my mother strode
down the gravel driveway
like a man.
And lying among rotten apples
held in baseball gloves of grass,
I think of roads that twist and turn
like some lunatic on a sleepless night
when the witch's moon illuminates select laurel leaves,
when I stretch to peer at brassy stars from my bed.
"Mama, I'm secretly in love with a poet,
and I've wanted to jump from Wiseman's View."

Tired from hoeing and weeding,
at equilibrium with life,
I know the aged earth-smell of cold breathing cellars,
the damp ground richly raisoned with chinkapins,
the mine shaft bleeding rust,
and the Indian sky, bruised and dying.

I can see myself searching
down Johnson's Hollow
between lost generations
of a mountain clan,
reading ominous letters
shaped by the tops of trees,
wanting to call mama,
wondering why I'm not satisfied,
when all I ask is for the thirst and the water.

Pauletta Hansel

Girl Villanelle

She's still there, that girl,
the one I was and hoped to leave behind.
I am forever loosening the ties.

The only life she could imagine for herself
was one she'd heard already in a song.
She's still there. That girl

took more than her share and left scattered
on the table all that could have fed her.
Hell-bent, she was, on loosening the ties.

I am not ready yet to claim her as my own.
She thought her body was the price of being seen.
She's still there, that girl,

bound and shivering inside her own smooth skin.
I'll say for her what she could not; that's how
I'm loosening the ties

and slipping through the doorway
from the past—I won't return alive.
Though she's still there, that girl.
Me, I'm loosening the ties.

Carrie Mullins

Excerpt from *Night Garden*

Old Cove Press, 2016; Reprinted by permission

It was too hard to be around Bobo when he was this way, so Marie went to the park to walk. Crawford Park was only a couple of blocks away from Bobo's house, and it had a walking track that went all the way around. Each lap was a quarter of a mile.

The park was nothing great. It was down in a bowl beside the quarry and had an amphitheater. Marie walked by a couple of kids mounding sand in the playground. She saw a wadded-up latex glove in the grass beside a trash can. She looped around down by the wooded area, where she could see the houses along Quarry Street. Four or five middle school boys sat on the back wall of the amphitheater. A BMX bike leaned against the wall and one of the boys kept moving the handlebars back and forth.

When Marie got close enough, she said hey and they said hey back to her. Then she said, "How are you all doing?" She heard her dad in her voice then, heard her dad acknowledging people, talking to people that he saw, whether he knew them or not. "Doing all right," one of the boys said.

As she walked around the curve of the walking track, she heard a girl on the grassy stage that probably had never been used for a play. The girl yelled that she needed a motherfucking lighter for her goddamned cigarette. Two boys standing beside her searched their pockets. Marie watched the girl. She was twelve, maybe thirteen. She wore a push-up bra under her printed tank top, shiny white basketball shorts that came down to her knees, and knock-off Air Jordans with hot pink soles.

Marie kept walking. She walked by the train tracks that rose up ten or fifteen feet above the park. The tracks came out of the quarry and circled round to make part of the bowl that formed the park. When she got to the playground again, the girl was riding one of the bikes around. She had blue-green hair. Everyone in the park watched her. The couples who sat on top of the picnic tables under the shelter watched her. Some older girls and a boy on the basketball court watched her. She was like a magnet, even Marie couldn't help herself.

The girl moved to the swings and the boys followed her and all of them swung for a while. When she jumped off the swing, her small body floated in the air, hair flowed behind, until she landed on her knees and jumped back up.

The girl got back on the bike. One of the boys followed her. They rode across the basketball court, through the half-court game the older girls played. The girl turned so sharp at the midcourt line she made the boy wreck into her, their bikes made a metal tangle on the concrete, the boy momentarily underneath it all. The girl stood up unhurt and laughed down at the boy.

Then Marie saw the blue and yellow of the CSX engine, up above all of them, as it moved out of the quarry. The cars on the train were weirdly new, weirdly clean and unscratched, all painted the same dark brown color with white letters on the side. They were full of gravel. She'd never seen numbers and letters that clear and crisp on the side of a train.

The train was moving slow and when the horn sounded all the people in the park put their fingers in their ears, but not that girl. It was like her already amped-up body got another spark lit in it. She grabbed the boy's arm and they ran through the grass, past the picnic shelters, through the sand of the playground area, up the scrubby hill to the tracks, right up to the moving train.

They stood so close to the train, it made Marie clench her fists. She fought the urge to yell at her to get back down and away from there. She willed the girl back down the hill, back into the bowl of the park. But the girl didn't come back. She started to run beside a car and grabbed one of the metal bars that went up the side of the car like a ladder. She stood on one bar and held onto another until she disappeared from view.

Part of Marie wanted to grab that same bar and be up there with her, moving on down the track to wherever that train was going. Somewhere far away. She thought of how they could fall under those neat new wheels, under those neat new cars, all the weight of that gravel would push down on them, and the wheels would cut their bodies in half, let one half roll down the hill into some other park in some other town along the rail line, the other half roll down onto the highway. It would be quick. She was beginning to see the benefit of a quick death.

Marie sat on a bench where she could watch the rest of the cars roll by. The boy who had followed the girl acted like he was going to jump on the train too, but it was moving faster now. He stood back from the tracks and threw gravel at the last car on the train, then he jogged behind it down the track.

The girl must have hung on only as far as downtown Crawford because she came running back down the tracks, back down the scrubby hill into the park, back among the boys who were still sitting in the amphitheater. They were all loud now, the boys and this girl, sitting in the grass with their bikes beside them.

A police car pulled up. Marie heard the girl say, "Oh shit," and then saw her jump the fence of the track and take off through the trees. Marie watched her run up Quarry Street, run across a yard, and disappear into a small white house. The police officer talked to the boys and Marie tried to listen, to see what he was asking them. The boys were talking low, but she heard one of them say, "She went to my mammaw's house."

Marie wondered if she should have made the call to the police. She was old enough now to be someone's mother, she could be the mother of that girl someday. Maybe her baby, her daughter, would grow up to be that wild, that dangerous.

Christopher Petruccelli

Darlin Cory

She's a bum ditty banjo woman.
Has hammerclaws for hands.
She doesn't pick and roll,
instead, she strikes, strikes,
strikes each string, every vibration
shaking out the sounds of hollers,
and sweet southern scent
of summer singlins. She beats
the banjo's head as the moon
shines across the Watauga River.
Crystal waves twin—turn
the color of pitch pine and wisteria—
then break. The thump keg beats
its drum as the bum ditty woman
sings about the Muddy Mississippi
and we're two steppin, flat footin,
while she slaps the banjo
until we all fall down, dead.

Omope Carter Daboiku

You Are

You are under 30, born after vitality
had morphed to wisdom.
But, your *kujichagulia*
– the right to define yourselves –
is in full force, and not just at Kwanzaa time.
The royal "we" and "they"
describe you and your generation.

Your knees are not freezing in winter,
not red from exposure.
Biology does not define you
or the clothes you wear.
Your hair is not fried with heat or
conked with lye, seeking some false sense of beauty.

You are not asking, but demanding
that your Elders accept change.
I defied your grandmother, born in '32,
for pierced ears at fourteen.
I wonder how she would relate to your
pierced septum, natural hair and love choices?

You are under 30, and choice is your birthright.
You are free to sit or spend wherever you wish;
Yet, as hill children you know that spending
does not define who you are.

You are under 30 and I, your mam,
am twice thirty plus three.
I am the past, and you are the present.
You are the sculptors of our collective future,
pioneers blazing a new trail.

Blessed be.

Cecile Dixon

How the Parts Fit

"Yeeee-haaaawwww." The crowd screamed and people stomped on the boards above my head as number eleven, Tank Crawford intercepted a pass and ran with the ball twenty yards, first down for the Ingall Mountain Coal Miners. I wanted to scream with the hometown crowd, but it would be a dead give away to my hiding place under the bleachers. Everybody in town came to every football game. Wasn't much else to do on Fall Friday nights. Very few people really watched the game. Men traded knives, women traded gossip and kids like me, we played games. Tonight my friends, Janie, Billy, Danny, Tim and I were playing Fox and Hound but everybody paused whatever they were doing to cheer the high school football team on at the appropriate times. This time I didn't cheer. I kept quiet and peeked at the field through the wooden planks.

I heard shuffling sounds in the tall grass behind me. I crouched low and peered into the darkness. I saw Danny just about the time he saw me.

"Fox in the trap. I got you Bean," he yelled but not too loud.

"I give. Did you see Tank intercept that pass?" I asked as Danny wiggled into my hiding spot for a better look at the playing field.

"Aww, heck naw. I was back in Johnson's pasture chasing Tim. He got away, but then I found you."

I caught a whiff of Irish Spring soap smell as Danny moved closer for a better view. I breathed the scent in deep. I like Irish Spring. If I had to get found, I was glad it was Danny who found me. His arm brushed against my chest and I got a funny feeling down low, way down in the pit of my belly. Danny turned toward me. His face was right in front of mine. He ducked his head and our foreheads bumped, but not before his lips brushed mine. We looked at each other for a few seconds. I could see Danny's eyes. They looked funny, too big for his face. Suddenly he jumped up and ran off the way he had come, across Johnson's field. I licked my lips. They tasted like salt.

I sat right there in that spot, without moving until the game was over. I didn't even know if we won or lost. I sat there until I heard Mama hollering, "Bean. Bean. Beatrice Ann Murphy, come on. We're going home."

On the way home, in the darkness of the car's backseat, I rubbed my hand across my belly and wished I could feel that feeling again.

That night as I was brushing my teeth, I took a long hard look at my lips in the mirror. Nothing special about them, just lips. But these lips had been kissed by a boy. Not just any boy, an eighth grader. Danny.

Mama came into the bathroom to put clean towels on the shelf.

"Mama, do remember the first time you was kissed?"

Mama smiled a silly smile. "Well, yes."

"Do you remember what Daddy's lips felt like?"

"Who said it was your Daddy?" Mama laughed and swatted me with a clean towel.

"It wasn't Daddy?" I squealed, spitting toothpaste onto the mirror. "Who was it? How old were you? Did you like it?"

"Lord, it was a long time ago. I've forgotten all that mess. It's late, past your bedtime. Get on into bed." Mama quit smiling and acted all nervous. "Twelve years old is too young to be thinking about boys and kissing. There's a time for that when you're older."

It was the same thing she always said. I was too young.

I lay awake a long time, thinking about Danny and wondering who my mama kissed before my daddy and how old I'd have to be before Mama or somebody would tell me about boys and kissing.

The very next day, Saturday, I was sitting on the soda

pop chest at the gas station, waiting for my uncle Kenny to get his oil changed. Kenny spent a lot of time at Jimmy Ray's. He'd saved up two hundred dollars and bought an old Ford. It wouldn't start half the time, but Kenny acted like it was a Cadillac. He spent more time working on it with Jimmy Ray's tools than he spent driving it. He fussed and made me wipe my feet before I got in. Getting his driver's license last spring had warped his brain.

From my perch I saw Judy Parnell pull her little red car up to the gas pump. She climbed out of the car as Jimmy Ray came scurrying out of the dark garage bay. She was wearing a short shirt and jeans that hugged her hips real low. So low that her bellybutton was in plain view. I had never seen a woman show her bellybutton like that, in public, right in the middle of the day. Jimmy Ray began pumping her gas and they spoke a few words and laughed. Judy stood there watching as he pumped her gas. She put her left hand on her hip and cocked her lower body forward, like women sometimes do. Judy put her right hand on Jimmy's arm for just a second. He looked up at her and grinned. Judy smiled and walked to the gas station.

When Judy came through the door she made a beeline straight to the pop case. I slid down from my perch to allow her to choose a soft drink.

For something to say, I said, "Cokes in the front are hot. Jimmy just filled the case."

As she chose a cold drink from the back of the case she said "Thanks, I hate to grab a warm pop, especially on a hot day like today. Do you want one? My treat." She held out a second soda.

"Thanks," I replied as I took the pop and opened it on the lid pull.

I watched through the big window as she paid Jimmy Ray for the pop and gas, winking as she handed him the money. Jimmy Ray stared at her backside as she climbed into her car. When she pulled out onto the road he turned toward the station, still grinning like a possum in pokeberry time. In the girl's room at school, I overheard Brenda Warner talking about Judy. She said that Judy had a lot of boyfriends. A lot. Brenda said that Judy went out with a different man every night. Was Jimmy Ray one of Judy's boyfriends?

When the oil change was done, I rode with my Uncle Kenny to my grandparents' house. As we got out of the car my uncle began walking toward the barn. As usual I started tagging behind.

He turned to me and said, "You go on in the house. We're going to put that little mare to stud. It ain't no place for girls."

Without argument, I walked into the front door of the house and straight to the kitchen, where my grandma was cooking supper. She looked up as I walked out the back door. I was on a mission and didn't have time to chat. Like Nancy Drew in a mystery book, I circled around the out buildings in the back yard. I took cover along the tree line and made my way, hidden by the trees, to the side of the barn. Peering through the cracks between the worn boards I watched my grandpa lead the little red mare into the barn driveway. I could see the muscles of her flanks trembling. She seemed skittish and he spoke to her in a soft soothing voice. I couldn't make out his words because the stud horse was making so much racket. Even though I couldn't see him, I could hear him, snorting, pawing at the ground, and occasionally kicking the sides of his stall. When the little mare whinnied, he answered with a loud demanding cry.

Grandpa led the mare farther into the barn, out of my line of vision. I moved down the barn's side in the same direction, but a pile of hay on the other side of the barn wall blocked my vision. I stood on my toes and strained my neck trying to see around the hay, but the bales were stacked too thick and tall.

I heard my grandpa say, "Let him to her." As I heard the latch of the stall door slide open, the stud's cries became coarser and the mare's whinny became frantic, higher pitched, almost painful. Growing up on a farm, I was no stranger to the ways of animals. I had seen roosters top hens, and, once, I had once seen two hounds stuck together like someone had glued their privates, but nothing in my experience had prepared me for the raw, excited sounds I heard coming from that barn.

The voices of the horses became louder. There were a lot of shuffling and stomping sounds and every now and then, a loud bang like a hoof kicking at wood. I could hear the big stud snort. I frantically tried to find a spot where I could see, but to no avail. I was close enough to smell sweet horse sweat scent, but with only sounds, it was left to my imagination just what was truly happening on the other side of the hay. Did the stud top the mare, like a rooster, then fluff his coat like feathers? Did they stick together? Did the little mare have to drag the stud around the pasture for hours as she cropped the grass?

The men too had become more animated. I heard my grandpa say, "Watch him now. Don't let him bite her. She's worth more than two of him." My uncle was cursing under his breath and his voice sounded strained, as if he were lifting something heavy.

The stud began grunting, a sound I had never heard a horse make before. This was accompanied by a wet, smacking sound. After much commotion the little mare screamed, sounding more scared than I had ever heard an animal sound. Then there was a loud thump and it got quiet. Grandpa began his soothing chant again. I heard a stall bolt slide shut. The stud was still snorting but quieter, in rhythm with his fast breathing.

Grandpa came out of the barn leading the mare back to her pen. I flattened my body against the rough barn wall, praying he didn't turn around and see me. I tried to hold my breath, because for some reason it was coming loud and ragged, matching the tempo of the stud's. My heart was pounding in my chest and I had a funny feeling in my stomach, like I had done something much worse than just sneak off to the barn.

When grandpa was out of sight, I once again used the tree line for cover. As I returned to the kitchen, I began setting the table, without being told to.

As I placed the dishes, I replayed the barn sounds. I tried to picture what action could cause each of the sounds. The only picture my mind could see was that of the mare and stud, rearing up on their hind legs, playing patty-cake with their shod hooves. My spying had left me with more questions than before. Did the mare get a funny feeling in her belly, like I did when Danny kissed me?

The next morning I ate my pancake and got dressed for church. I tried to stay asleep. Reverend Alcorn's sermons were better if you could half sleep through them. It made you not watch the clock so much.

I took my place in the fourth pew on the right, wedged in between Mama and Grandma. The organ had begun to play and Grandma handed me a mint. As I was unwrapping it I heard a murmur and rustling toward the back of the church. Mama, Grandma and I turned to see what the commotion was about. The whole church was looking as Judy Parnell took a seat in a back pew. I was wide-awake now. All the church ladies bent their heads to each other. Their hat brims touching as they whispered to first one side then the other and nodded toward Judy. I'd never seen her in our church before. I didn't think she went to church. Maybe she didn't even pray.

Reverend Alcorn stepped to the podium. As he looked over the congregation, he spied Judy. His face got real red, like somebody had boxed both of his jaws. Quickly he looked down at the pulpit and spent a long minute fumbling with some papers. Finally, he led us in prayer. He didn't welcome Judy like he did most of the people who visited the Ingall Mountain, First Baptist Church. After the choir sang, the Reverend began preaching. He didn't even take time to warm up. He started right off waving his Bible in the air and thumping on the pulpit.

"It says in First Corinthians 6:18 'he that committeth fornication sinneth against again his own body.'"

I tried to ask Grandma what fornication was but she shushed me, whispering, "Hush, your Mama'll tell you when your old enough."

The Reverend preached on about fornication for the better part of an hour. I tried to look it up in Grandma's Bible, but it wasn't real clear. Seemed to me that fornication was a sin committed by both men and women. I sure hoped that somebody would tell me what it was before I committed it without knowing.

After eternity, the Reverend wound down and the deacons began to pass the collection plate. Now they skipped over Judy because the church board had decided that it wasn't right to ask visitors to give money to the church, only members. Judy made a little huffing sound and I twisted in my seat to see her wave a dollar toward Brother Blevins. He ignored her and walked up the aisle. Grandma tapped my leg and made me turn around.

The deacons had finished up the collecting and was almost ready to set the brass plate on the alter, when the sound of quick walking came from the center isle. It was Judy. She had a mad look on her face and with each step her titties bounced. It was hard not to miss the fact that she wasn't wearing a bra and her nipples poked at the thin fabric of the dress she was wearing.

She marched straight up the aisle and just as Brother Silas was setting the plate down, she carefully unfolded a bill she was holding in her hand. Looking straight up into the Reverend's eyes she carefully laid the bill into the collection plate. When she bent over the fabric of her dress pulled tight over her bottom. A large yellow smiley face grinned at the congregation from the backside of her underwear. The thin, pale blue, dress fabric couldn't hide it. Reverend's face turned blotchy red and he mumbled something I couldn't make out. I stood up to get a better view of what Judy put in the plate and Grandma jerked me back to my seat. But not before I got my first glimpse of a hundred dollar bill. Judy fast walked back to where she'd been sitting. Her lips were pulled tight and she didn't look right or left, just straight ahead.

I have been going to the First Baptist Church since I was born. I go to prayer meeting and Wednesdays and then twice on Sunday. The Reverend baptized me when I was eight years old. I know how things work at church. It always goes along the same, Sunday after Sunday, the same. But not today. This Sunday people whispered and shifted in their seats to look back at Judy. The women worked their fans double time, although it weren't no hotter than usual. The Reverend cut his closing prayer quick and didn't even ask for prayer requests. As soon as the Amen, I ducked under Grandma's arm and headed out of the church.

Judy was striding across the parking lot as I cleared the church house door. She opened the door of her car and grabbed a pack of cigarettes from the dash. She slammed the door and leaned against the hood before lighting up. Taking a long drag of smoke, she closed her eyes before exhaling slowly.

I stopped dead in my tracks, trying to think of something to say to her. As I stood there thinking, Grandpa walked past me. He walked right in front of Judy on his way to his pick-up.

"Glad to see you at service, Judy," he said.

Judy laughed a snorting laugh and said, "I guess you're bout the only one."

Grandpa walked on to his truck and rolled down the windows, so the truck would cool down while he waited on Grandma to get done congregatin. I wanted to ask Judy about the hundred-dollar bill. Where she got it and why she gave that much money to the church offering. But I knew better. It wasn't polite to talk to people about money.

So instead I said, "The Reverend shore preached a good one

today didn't he?"

"I guess that depends on which side of his sermon you were sitting. I think that he's been saving that one up, just for me."

I was pondering what Judy meant by that when Mama and Grandma came out of the church door. Grandma saw me standing by Judy and stretched her arm out long and crooked her pointer finger at me.

"I got to go. Grandma wants me," I said as I began to walk away. "Bye."

"Later," Judy mumbled.

When I got to Grandma, she Mama and several of the church ladies had their heads bent together talking low. As I waited to see what Grandma wanted, I heard Ms. Peters say, "The Reverend went out there to read some Bible and pray with her, just being a good Christian, he was, and she all but slammed the door in his face. But not before using some awful, vulgar language."

Grandma noticed me standing on the steps, she said, "We are talking grown folks' talk. Go on and play."

"But you motioned for me," I replied. I was kind of mad cause she had interrupted my talk with Judy for nothing.

"Ain't no but about it. I just didn't want you where you had no business." She turned back to the little cluster of churchwomen.

I saw Judy leaving the parking lot as I wandered among the cars, thinking about what she said about the Reverend's sermon. I always thought the preachin was for everybody, not just one person.

I wandered over to where my Uncle Kenny was talking with a group of his friends. I sneaked up behind them. I hid behind a red pick-up, trying not to get dust on my Sunday dress, as I strained my ears to eavesdrop. The boys were laughing and poking each other in the ribs.

"Did you see what she was wearing?"

"I'd like to…." Loud laughter and shoulder punches.

"Her name's on the pisser wall at Jimmy Ray's."

"I seen that. Says for a good time call her. I wrote down the number."

"Did you call her?"

"I'm going to. Maybe as soon as I get home."

"Yeah right. You're too chicken."

"I bet I know how she got that hundred dollars."

They were talking about Judy. I edged closer so I could hear better.

Uncle Kenny saw me, "Bean, get out of here. Go on and play with the little girls. Get now." He kicked gravel at me.

"You ain't the boss of me. I'll go anywhere I want to." He was always acting like he was a king, especially now, since he was a high school senior.

"Don't make me get a switch," he threatened.

"You hit me and Grandpa will beat you with a trace line." All the boys laughed. "I'm leavin not cause you're making me, but cause I got better things to do than hang around you." More laughter from the boys as I walked away, scuffing the shine on my patent leathers in the gravel.

After church we went to my grandparents' for dinner. We went to their house every Sunday after church. That was another thing that didn't change. We ate fried chicken every Sunday at my grandparents'. I'm glad I love fried chicken. After dinner, the same as every Sunday I helped Grandma wash dishes. She washed and I dried.

"You awful quiet today, Bean. Something bothering you?" Grandma handed me a teacup.

"No Mam, nothing wrong. I'm just thinking." I dried the cup and stretched up to put it on the shelf.

"Thinking about a lot of things or just one thing?"

"They's a lot of things, but they all seem tied to one thing." I took a handful of silverware and dried the water from each piece.

"Don't push so hard to grow up. It'll come in its own sweet time."

"I don't want to grow up. I just want to know things."

I rubbed a spoon real hard. "Bout boys and such."

"Some things you'll know, when you're growed enough." Grandma dried her hands on the dishtowel. "Boys are after one thing, till a certain age. Maybe they don't ever change. Girls are after something else. They just don't know it."

"Grandma, how old are you?"

"Fifty-seven. Why?"

"Well, I was thinkin it's been a long time since you was my age."

Grandma laughed so hard tears ran down her face. She wiped them off with her apron and laughed some more. Right then I came to the conclusion that my grandma and my mama didn't know anything about sex. Even if they had Daddy and Grandpa. Even if they had kissed a hundred boys and birthed babies. If they ever knew they had surely forgot.

After the dishes were done and Grandma quit laughing I shoved an apple into my pocket and walked out into the pasture. The little mare was there, munching on what was left of the fall clover. I looked her over carefully. She didn't look any different than she had when Grandpa led her into the barn. I held the apple out to her and she gently took it from my hand.

'It's a shame you can't talk," I said to the mare. "Cause I got a feelin that you know more about sex than Grandma and Mama put together." I remembered something Daddy always said, *If you want to build a barn, don't ask a guitar player how to do it.* I needed an expert.

The next day I decided to walk out the road past Judy's trailer. Maybe I might chance to see her. As an excuse I tied a rope-leash on my cur dog, Blue. This was an unusual occurrence for Blue and he fought the leash, tugging away, doing flips and sometimes just sitting down. Instead of walking him, I was dragging him.

When I dragged Blue past Judy's trailer her red car was in the drive. The trailer windows were open and I could hear country music coming from inside. Walking slowly I scanned the trailer and yard looking for any sign of Judy. She was nowhere outside and peering with all my might I was unable to see into the darkness beyond the open windows.

I continued on around the curvy road for about a half-mile just to make my pretense of walking Blue believable to anyone who might question my motives. When I passed the trailer on my return, Judy's car was gone and the trailer was silent. I felt disappointed as I took the rope off Blue's neck and set him free to find his way home.

I repeated Blue's walk every day for the next three days without any success. Each day the drive was empty. During that time I searched the streets of town at every opportunity for signs of Judy, or her little red car. I was beginning to get worried. Maybe she had been kidnapped and was being held hostage by some evil city slickers. With me being the only one to notice that she was missing, I would have the responsibility of rescuing her.

On the fourth day Blue didn't put up too much fight as I tied the rope around his neck. He seemed resigned to the walk, even if he couldn't see any reason in it.

When I rounded the curve by Judy's trailer, I could hear Bocephus' voice blaring away. Judy was in the drive washing her little car, applying soapy water with a rag, stretching to scrub the roof. As she strained to reach the farthest part of the car's roof, the cut off shorts she was wearing showed the round bottom of each butt cheek. I had never seen so much skin shown by a grown woman, out in the open, where anybody might drive by. I was so scandalized and fascinated by her short shorts and white bikini-top that I almost forgot to be relieved that she hadn't been kidnapped.

Blue, having grown used to being set free at this point in our walk picked that moment to start fighting against the rope. Twisting, yelping and tugging he slipped the noose over his head.

As I stood there with the rope in my hand, watching

Blue hightail toward home, I heard Judy ask, “Do you need some help catching your dog?”

“No.” I replied. “He’ll find his way home.”

Trying to think of something to keep our talk going I asked, “Can I get a drink of water from your hose?”

“Sure,” she said, extending the running hose toward me.

I hadn’t really thought I was thirsty until I touched the water to my lips and found my mouth was as dry as dust. I drank deep gulping swallows from the hose as Judy continued washing her car. After I drank my fill I used the hose to rinse the soapy bubbles off the car.

“It’s awful dirty,” I said.

“Settin behind Jimmy Ray’s, waiting on a clutch, sure didn’t do the wax any good,” Judy replied as she scrubbed at dried bird crap.

I felt a little let down that her absence was as simple as a worn out clutch. Getting kidnapped was much more exciting.

For lack of anything else to say, I replied, “I’ve heard he’s a good mechanic.”

“Yeah, he’s kept this thing on the road for me. I’ve seen you walking by here a lot lately, what ya been up to?”

I turned away so she couldn’t see the guilt on my face as I lied. “I just been walking Blue, to get away and think.”

“What’s been on your mind, that requires so much thinkin?”

I continued spraying water on the car as I thought about my answer.

“Oh, boys and stuff like that.”

She turned toward me, pausing with the rag in her hand. “How old are you? she asked as she eyed me up and down.

“Thirteen,” I lied for the second time. Teenagers know a lot more about sex than twelve-year-olds.

“Ain’t you Luke and Jelly’s girl?”

"Yeah, I'm Bean," I answered, praying that she wasn't planning on talking to my parents.

Taking the hose from my hand she gave the car a once over before shutting off the water. Sitting down on the trailer steps, she lit a cigarette as she patted the step beside her. I joined her as she took a long drag.

Exhaling the smoke into the sunny evening air she said, "Is that why you been coming by here every day? Are you looking for answers that nobody will give you?"

I nodded a guilty yes. As I tightened the laces of my gym shoes I mumbled, "My mama told me about getting my period and how that means I'm becoming a woman, but she didn't tell me what it means to be a woman." I paused a seeming eternity working up my courage. "You know, about sex and boys and stuff. I really don't think she knows much about it. She seemed real nervous when she talked to me. When I asked Grandma, she just says that I am a youngun and them things will come in time." I continued tying and re-tying my shoelaces.

Judy laughed a musical, tinkling laugh. "Well, my friend, you are wrong. Your mama and grandma know all about sex. They've just forgotten about men. That happens sometimes with women. They get tied up taking care of kids and working jobs and they forget to treat their men special. Sex is no big mystery. It's just certain body parts that fit together. The mystery lies in the dance between men and women."

"You mean like holding hands and kissing? Is that the dance you are talking about, like you winking at Jimmy Ray?" I asked, trying hard to make sense out of her words.

She grinned. "You sure notice a lot, don't you? Yeah, me winkin at Jimmy Ray is part of the dance. Men, and boys like to think that they are special; like everything they do or say is the most interesting thing you ever saw or heard, even if they told you the same thing ten times before. Don't get me wrong now, all men are interested in sex. It's just that they like the challenge of trying to get sex almost as much as the sex itself. If you treat them like they are interesting and entertaining, they think they just might be able to get in your britches. Do you understand what I'm sayin?"

"I think so. Sex begins before a man and woman ever touch each other. Like when my daddy tells my mama that she is pretty and she giggles," I said, my voice betraying amazement that Judy found the subject seemed so simple and easy to talk about.

"You catch on fast," Judy replied as she tossed her cigarette butt into the gravel drive. "I got things to do. You go on home now and if you have questions ask your mama. She'll tell you how those body parts fit together when she thinks the time is right. Don't blame her if she acts nervous. She's just worried that her words will come out wrong. People make too much out of sex. It's been done since ole Adam and Eve, you'd think that they'd have figured out how to talk about it by now." Judy stood and stepped into her trailer.

I walked home that night feeling like a grown up woman, even if I still didn't know how the parts fit.

Juanita Mays

relinquish the title

of miss nice
do your best
help everybody
good daughter
answer to
dissolving shadow
creature who paces
girl tricked by time
carry words upon your back
mysterious speeches
from antique hatboxes
spill them over the city
print your secrets on music sheets
blowing in the wind
toss this new language
into the middle of your dreams
insist upon your beliefs
feed upon blood-truth
and the red meat of hungry lions
then when night is dark
refuse to charm
with the grey steel stare of eyes
something has been stolen
something you would never give away
release the past
cross the bridge of winter limbs
and with each breath
breathe nearer to your god.

Susan Underwood

God as My Great Aunt Lucy, Tutoring Me in Botany

I had seen the trilliums but had not known:
their name such a trinity of poise,
bride-white petals in their prime blushing to pink,
by the start of May shriveled brown,
quick as tinder in the first hot hours.

She leaned her tall old body beside my young head.
I felt her in my head, beside my damp curls,
her glasses in my periphery, her splotched fingers
naked inside the pale petals.

I knew her mystery, that she'd never married,
without any answer she might have told,
only old in a way others were not old.
In her house of books floor to ceiling,
she slept alone in her tilted bedroom
sinking into the habits of a cold house
and got up in the blue-black dawn
to drive to school and teach science.

She knew the slow, private numeral of each season,
the flower's way of saying itself in threes.
She could tell I didn't believe a simple flower could count.
Three leaves, she showed me, repeating
the awkward, beloved words of a kingdom she knew—
three stigmas, three sepals and petals
and bracts, the stamens in groups of three.

The lightness I touched, the trillium's
satin math, put right the light
through the trees all over again,
light on the bell of bloom I touched like a face upturned.
We raised up and walked further along the trail
into those woods beautiful without voices,
and all around us, and upon us,
the lonely calculus of pollen lit its yellow reason.

Amy McCleese

For My Men

There isn't much to do on a Friday
if you overhear the counselor saying
there's nothing ahead for you, knowing
she thinks you'll end up working for pennies
with busted knuckles, thick-fingered,
like the men who raised you.
You can't leave the town
where your name is a badge,
spending your years proving
all those fuckers wrong.
No, for now.

I cannot blame you
for taking the Buick and a bat,
for crushing mailbox after mailbox
under starlight, up and down
hourglass roads while
the moon and cicadas stare.
you keep it quiet, inside,
perfecting the throwing
of a Budweiser up and over
your car onto a stop sign,
a satisfying metal crash.

Sherry Cook Stanforth

Just seeing a man about a dog

was Papa John's reply when I asked where he might be heading. Then he'd pretend to snatch my nose, spit some juice and walk off without answering why. After the flush, he'd come in smiling and give me back my nose. Daddy says it, too, from time to time—*just seeing a man about a dog*—so I try this phrase on my own daughter. "What?" she asks, when I give her a big wink and go off to finish my business. Once I return, she still doesn't get it. "What dog? What man?" rolling her eyes at my laughter, even when I remind her that we old-timers know how to spin metaphors just like the Bard, or rappers.

Then a scrap of story comes to mind, told once by my daddy on a cicada night when I was grown enough to hear it. So I ask her, do you want to know its sharp edge, too? Picture a man and a boy crossing the mountain to Dahlonega, wind beating through the truck cab, a pouch of Red Man chew sliding over the dash with Great-Great Papa John bellowing "I Am a Pilgrim" and hair-pinning around all the curves of Union County, Georgia. On that day, the boy—her grandpa—is riding shotgun and staring down sheer rock faces into the void. He's just moved back from Ohio to stay a little while, until a few things get figured out. The ride dizzies him. He drinks RC Cola and drops in peanuts because Papa John says it will help. I tell her how I can see those two bumping along the laurel tunnels and finally pulling into the rutted yard—chickens running every which way and a girl drooped against the porch rail, holding tight to a milk bucket, flinging corn.

They climb out and stand before the broken down blue house all webbed in trumpet vine and flanked by a rusted out oil drum and a doorless Chevy. Dogs creep out snarling and then a fella rounds the corner to holler them back into the weeds. He snaps the hatchet he's been using right into the dirt without even looking up, and that's when Papa John sends

Daddy off into the yard to play. The girl, someone a nine-year-old boy surely doesn't want to know too well, follows. The men hang around the stoop talking the weather, haggling over the price of a coonhound.

In a blink, Daddy got the idea of pointing over to the outhouse, and he told that girl he needed to *go see a man about a dog*. Didn't want one thing to do with her—he even pretended to bang the door shut, then he lit out for the creek, trying his best to fool her. But she tracked him down like a panther, found him out. They skipped rocks and hunted for crawdads, daring each other to cross chestnut logs, smarting off about who knew this and that, and who was the best runner and climber—then came the shout. They headed back toward the house and that's when the man came at her, ground hornet mad and shaking his fist about a thing she'd done wrong. She'd let go some chore or had gone and made some intolerable mess. He lifted her right up by the neck of her dress and yanked her across the yard, kicking her backside so that she flew over a stump. Then he caught her again, this time by the arm, and knocked her straight up the steps. She limped into the dark house without ever looking back or making a sound.

After a spell, Papa John said he might do a little bit of thinking, then stop in on Tuesday, but his eyes held the no deal look when they shook hands. He motioned for Daddy to get into the truck. The man cut a plug of tobacco, watching while they drove around the back end of the shed and stirred up a commotion of barking. But the ride back home over the mountain—it's dead quiet, with no coon dog to stand behind in the truck bed, flapping its tongue and ears into the wind. I tell her it was a time when they could find no words for the business a man might have, and what a man might lose if he didn't take proper care. Then, I snatch her nose away and quick, before she can say anything, I give it back.

William Graham

Scrap yard

From whatever can be found
salvage the wreckage and build.

Assemble a home
with broken boards
rusted tin
bent nails
old car seats
and an eager hammer.

Swing furiously.

Andrew Jensen

build me

i'm disassembled.
the parts of me are as separate as they were
when they were shipped on the sea grayer than stormclouds,
when they were carried through the land bluer than clear skies,
all the way to the first house my parents ever shared.

my mother and my father put my parts together
at that very first house,
a farmhouse sitting on a fraction of an acre
on which they grew grass
to harvest every few weeks.

on a sweaty summer sunday,
my mother and my father
built me in the dark, moldy garage
where the sun could barely reach,
insufficiently for its assets
but sufficiently for its liabilities.
my mother flipped the switch
to the fluorescent bulbs overhead.
their cool white light only magnified the heat.
my father opened his rusty robin's-egg blue toolbox,
where wrenches and ratchets oozed in spilled sludge.

he had built two boys before,
but my mother had never made a kid.
still she labored with him in that thick, dull heat,
as bugs buzzed along with the flickering fluorescent,
and she figured out where all the body parts went.

neither kept track of how many hot hours passed—
assembling a skeleton alone is horrifying work.
the spine, skull, ribs, and limbs take shape with no effort—
it's those dumb little ones that'll get you.

next, you got to wire the frame with nerves and veins,
pad the bones with muscle.
nuzzle those organs in there somehow
without bursting one of them.
run the veins through,
and then sit and wait
till all the blood in the carton is finally funneled in.
when that's all done is when the real fun begins.
the skin isn't sewn on in sections,
you have to stretch it all over the whole body in one piece.

just imagine my parents' frustration
when, after collapsing on the couch
in the irritated, exhausted relief
that always seems to follow a day in the garage,
they had to undo and then redo that entire process
because they forgot to first put my brain in my skull.

sometimes i wonder if my father,
still only half as crafty as his own father,
instead found a way
to jimmy my brain into my skull through my skin.
i wouldn't put it past him.

just imagine my parents' frustration
when, though they rebuilt me and maintained me with care,
i regularly fall apart screw by screw,
clanging on the hardwood floor in my room.

my grandpa said some machines just break down,
no matter how skilled the hands that build them,
no matter how much maintenance you give them,
no matter much you try to fix them.

Matthew S. Parsons

Green

I got my pay stub today, but I still can't feel the weight of a hammer the way my daddy can. I've seen him drive a metal spike in one punch. I've seen him carry three bags of shingles at once up a two-story building on an old, rusty, beat-to-hell extension ladder with nothing but God to hold it up against the wind.

He told me that when you stop missing nails, your pecker stops growing. Then he said he missed them on purpose every now and then just to see. It hasn't worked for me yet, but I don't feel so bad anymore that I strike a big wood plank like lightning—never in the same place twice.

I took to squaring up the floor hoists with a big sledgehammer yesterday. It was a big old time, watching the wall come down. I'd seen it done, and I knowed it was out of square, so I give it a heave and it kind of crawled back into place. Well, all of it except the wall. Turns out that was just up for looks, because it had been nailed about as many times as I had and it wasn't hardly strong enough to have the foundation shift under it.

Daddy just laughed and asked me what the hell I thought I was doing. I told him I was bringing it up to square. He told me I wasn't bringing nothing up. He also said he wasn't either, and went back and opened a beer in the camper. He brought me up all right.

Matt Prater

Meditation at Cedar Branch

As some have said of Carolina's lights,
brown orbs above the ridges of Catawba—
orbs which echo all the lacrimae rerum,
this hillside still remembers its entrenchments:
all of the ones, under all of the various flags,
who died in snow-logged wool
beneath the gaze of God and Hannibal,
whose grand beasts, winged and tusked,
they saw (as if the fiery sword of Eden
was in their teeth) as new inventions
(ridged bullets, amputator's saws)
pierced them at the sternum
or at Achilles' tender root.

Again it is Antietam in late winter,
and my sinews are fine and masculine,
and I am back in this earth once again,
in magic hour's gold, exemplary light—
that one small hour of evening when the sky
has pulled itself against itself like a sheet fort,
and the sharp final light of evening skips
over the west ridge of mountains
like polished rocks spun on an eddy,
toward the blanket of yellow clouds
over the little ridge below.

I walk toward the lichened memento mori,
and the light on those stones is pure
buttercream, the light to the north
a canopy of Richmond grey draping
obelisks to the Confederate dead.
Each one is turned toward the East
for Christ's return; each is adorned
with coffee cans of faux poinsettia,
until left unattended in that year
the last of that old family who
kept Decoration Day has died.

Izzy Broomfield

exile

i spent ten years fetishizing Appalachia
land of mountains and roots
four seasons, snow and silence

land of the family farm
where my great aunt hung herself
land that was eminent domained to bury nerve gas
land of far more than pain and loss—

all of this i missed
from the blighted coastal plain
          an exile against my will
          that ached to be over

my homecoming, cut short
too queer, too manic, too different
too excited to be here
to be here

kicked out by the gatekeepers
defenders of the order
havers of power and doers of harm
in exile again weeks after my return

but to know people and to be known
to share memories and space and place
to be bound by something more than happenstance—

community
like breaking a fast
        it stoked my fire like only
        the end of absence can

i've looked out across both edges of this continent and into the unknown
i've learned much by leaving
but my heart ached to return

Lyn May

Home Sweet

I am ten years old, digging through my mother's pocketbooks looking for spare change to fill my piggy bank. I find little treasures like flavored lip gloss and gel-pens, a few earrings missing their matches. There are crinkled receipts for birthday presents on layaway and gas station purchases. Gallon of milk, gallon of gas, and a pack of Salem Slim 100s are all the same price: about four dollars, Mom says. She would be home after last call, wearing leather boots and a sequined top. She hates bartending, but the tips are decent, she says. Soon she will find work at Dawahares, the department store, and quit bartending.

My great grandmother, I call her Mawmaw, wakes around nine o'clock in the morning and I make her coffee: Maxwell House instant with just enough milk to turn the color. The cabinet is filled with old jam jars and white tea cups; dust has settled in the corners. I empty the sink into the dishwasher and start a load of towels. The linoleum floor is already warm this morning. The sun peeks through the white lace curtains of the kitchen window. There's a stack of bills on the table, stamped and ready to go off to wherever they go to be paid. Mawmaw told me what to write on the checks because, "I can't write too good anymore," she says. I collect the envelopes and walk barefooted across green carpet to the wooden front porch, down the steps and towards the walkway, which is cracked from over a decade's use. The gravel driveway is worn and needs replenishing. I raise the red flag on the mailbox and turn back to the doublewide. The Hatfields live next door, and often Connie sits out on her porch swing. "Don't play in the Hatfield's yard," Mawmaw says. "They're real particular." Aunt Von's old trailer sits on the other side with weeds so high you can't get to the front porch. A place you might call snake heaven. Precious, Mawmaw's blue heeler, sits on the top step of the porch, tongue hanging out. The creek whispers behind me and the breeze is subtle and quiet. The sun is coming through the clouds, nourishing the rose bush next to the walkway.

Pawpaw Charles found that bush on the side of the road one day about fifteen years ago, and decided Mawmaw should have it. The roses were the purest of white, Mawmaw says. Pawpaw pulled over and dug up the bush and hauled it home in his pick-up. The following blooming season, the bush was red and so was Pawpaw's face with anger. It's bloomed red every year since.

"He never once called me a bad name," she tells me. Pawpaw was a hard-working Italian man, the type "they just don't make anymore." He came to America with his parents and brothers from Naples, Italy. He passed away when my mother was young.

I sit down on the porch steps with Precious for a moment and hear the cars bend around the mountain above the holler. Hindsight tells me some are en route to work, others are just passing through or packed up to leave.

I know now this isn't a place where people move to, it's a place people leave behind. If you're born here, you stay here until you graduate high school and you either join the mines or the Marines. Many can't wait to get out, like my mother who has found her place oceanside. Many, like my father, regret they ever left and spend the rest of their lives trying to get back. Back to the rich warmth provided by familiarity. Of communities clustered together like black-eyed Susans. Houses are cheap and the cost of living is low, but the job market is scarce with opportunity. There is no room to blossom. I always wanted to live there with Mawmaw in Mingo County, West Virginia, but my father had higher hopes for me. I would go to college instead of becoming a miner's wife or a teenage mother. I would have the opportunity my mother and father decided to put on hold.

My mother tells me stories of learning how to drive on Buffalo Mountain, the one with turns so tight you almost have to hold your breath to make them. She grew up on the property Mawmaw still lives on. She used to go lay in the tanning bed after softball practice, and sometimes she wore combat boots and frayed denim with lots of purple eye shadow. She pulls an album off of Mawmaw's shelf to give me photographic proof. "Hey, it was the eighties," she says. Her hair is thick and permed into tight springs.

My father grew up in Chattaroy, West Virginia, just a twenty minute drive from Delbarton. He's told me stories of playing in the woods on the mountainside until it got so dark that his mom and Granddad would work themselves into a deep worry. "This time of year, it gets dark awful fast in the woods. The sun just drops and it's gone. You've got to be careful," is what Granddad would tell my dad after coming in too late one night, with crying younger brother in tow. My dad would move with his mother and brother to North Carolina in 1989.

The sun is out now, the air thick and humid in the middle of December. I make a point to sit on the porch a while when I'm here. This time, I'm visiting over winter break and will soon return to Asheville, North Carolina to begin another semester of college. There are puddles at the end of the driveway from yesterday's showers, thick with mud. I hear Mawmaw up and about inside so I join her. She's made herself a sandwich and is now resting her back on the couch. Her back is curved and crooked like the blue bulging veins in her hands. She closes her eyes and I imagine she is dreaming of days when she was in better health, on less medication. Her hair is chin-length and dove white from raising eight children and many grandchildren. I imagine she thinks of Pawpaw. I imagine being ten again, asking her to tell me stories she'd already told me dozens of times. When we talk on the phone now, she asks me, "When are you coming home?" I never know how to answer her, so I ask her to tell me a story. Sometimes it's the one about her carrying a gun on her when she was twelve years old and had to take the bus to work everyday. Sometimes it's the one about when she and Pawpaw decided to get married. I feel like a bee swarming a hollyhock trying to pull every detail into my memory so I can hold them, sweet as honey, for much longer than the time I have left with her.

I've known this holler my whole life. My knees still hold scars from being gravel-skinned twelve years ago. The backyard is where I saw my first copperhead. I was sitting in the living room of this trailer when we all found out Mawmaw Charlene, my mom's mother, had a heart attack and passed away days later. She is buried behind Burch High School, in the Cisco family cemetery. Airport Bottom is where I learned about pride, where I learned about death. When I return to West Virginia to visit with my family now, I am reminded of blasted mountains, coal dust, and cracked foundations. Somewhere under the landscape tinged grey, I still smell the honeysuckle on the creek bank. I still see the honey-glazed evening light that made me feel like I was apart of a scene from some movie. I hold these little things close to my heart so that it will always feel full.

When it is time to return for classes, I will hug Mawmaw. My aunt with comment on the weight I've lost. My mother will comment on how much taller I am than her. She will tell me to be careful on the mountain, that you can't hardly see for shit through the fog. I will pull out of the driveway and join the line of those just passing through. I will daydream about sitting on Mawmaw's porch in Delbarton, listening to the high creek after a storm, bullfrogs and crickets at dusk, the spectrum of season changes sprinkling across the mountainside. Perhaps I am a black- eyed Susan destined to return for only short seasons at a time.

Dale Marie Prenatt

Slaw Dog

Uncle pulled his oversize truck up
to an A&W root beer stand. *Here,*
we'll stop for something and get back on the road
before old Suzie gets to bothering everybody
up and down the holler wondering after us. Uncle bellowed

that he'd *Take a couple of plain dogs with a Coke float,*
you know, still with some West Virginia at the insides of his Os
but with a Midwest effect on the ends of his sentences.
After Grandma ordered, I stepped up hungry. And glad
to be included on a journey to a new place

where nobody knew me except these, who loved me,
and also Aunt Suzie. We'd only been out of the mountains four hours
or so and I'd only been about eight years old when, in an octave as high
as our latitude and a drawl as long as our four-lane
I asked for a *Slaw dog with sauce.*

The woman in the plastic hair net hadn't ever heard a voice like that.
She'd never taken an order like that and she didn't understand the words
I spoke when I said that. So she asked me again
what it was that I wanted to eat and I said louder, in a higher pitch
and slower, *Thank you, a slaw dog please. With sauce.*

She'd been working on the side of the highway for years
and so you'd expect that she would know how some people eat
chili sauce and creamy slaw on our weenies. Uncle sure remembered.
He lumbered up as fast as his round belly'd allow,
capped his palm on my tiny shoulder and began to laugh,

but in a way, I noticed, that wasn't his own.
His laugh sounded like he was embarrassed. Or ashamed.
She's asking for a chili dog, honey, with coleslaw, he said to the woman.
And he didn't wait for her to answer as he knelt down on one knee
to instruct me that *They don't make them like that here.*

He'd been out of the mountains four decades or so, sent away
by his daddy to never have to know a coal dark day
in an underground mine. And Uncle'd done fine at Ford
all this time. Always with a new truck and those boats and ATVs
and Harleys and Huskies and the boys, and Aunt Suzie.

He choked out another chuckle toward the woman in the hairnet
in the window by the highway. He said, *She's from West Virginia*
and ordered mine the same as his. Kicking my feet in the dirt,
I ate it all – his plain dog, his Sorry, his shame.
I'm sorry, he said. *She's from West Virginia.*

Maggie Naas

Blackberry Winter

Blackberry Winter
My grandmother told me the old people used to say
Cedar, the shavings we made and we browned the bread
Red-headed preacher-man with a mason jar of communion wine

Unseasonably cold
My young girls wrapped spring jackets
I don't make nothing no more
I sleep in on Sundays

Russ asked if I would ever go back
But the question becomes null
I'll always struggle to remember
Or willfully forget

Like there was something that got in my blood when I was a child
Of course I'll chase romantic ideas of simplicity
Even though I've forgot the recipe
I'll want for cornbread and another sip of wine

Nicole Rahe

defining popularity

when I moved out of Bethel-Tucky
classmates told me where I lived
had made me part of the un-in crowd

my Daddy's deer hanging limp
in the garage was a neon sign
no city folk lived here

Arwen Careaga

23

The Lord is my shepherd; I shall not want.
I was tortured by the 23rd Psalm
He maketh me to lie down in green pastures:
She was old for a teacher—black hair, black dress, hook nose
he leadeth me beside the still waters.
I saw her once in the grocery store and it was surreal
He restoreth my soul:
"What's she doing here?" I thought. "Teachers don't shop."
he leadeth me in the paths of righteousness for his name's sake.
Third grade. I was in the third grade.
Yea, though I walk through the valley of the shadow of death,
And she hated our accents.
I will fear no evil: for thou art with me
West Virginia accent on Kentucky hill mouths.
thy rod and thy staff they comfort me.
ENUNCIATE!
Thou preparest a table before me
Waaaaahnt not won't
in the presence of mine enemies:
Ehhhhhg not aaaaayyyygg
thou anointest my head with oil;
OY-ull
thou anointest my head with oil

Ulll is not a thing!
thou anointest my head with oil
OY-ull not Ullllll! BOY-ullll not buuuullllll!
my cup runneth over.
Don't sound ignernt
Surely goodness and mercy shall follow me
You don't want people thinking you don't know how to talk
all the days of my life:
We're going to do this until you all say it right
and I will dwell in the house of the Lord for ever.

Amen.

Michaela Miller

City

I come here
and eat 99 cent
french fries
and all I want
is fresh off the
rod iron
potato cakes.
I smell sewer,
and a waft
through the air
that reeks
of dog food,
when all I want
to smell is
honeysuckle in heat,
and Mamaw's eucalyptus
candle.
I feel bitter breezes
and the tag of my
sweater scratching
my neck,
when all I want
to feel is a
tattered quilt,
and elder arms
around me.

Joyce Compton Brown

Fourth Grade Civics Lesson

So Gail came back to school when her daddy had to sell his farm and she could make the big spinner twirl faster and faster and she pushed and ran and ran then jumped on and we laughed and laughed and held to the cold handles and I got mud on my new coat with the lambswool collar the best coat I'd ever had and not homemade. Gail's old bluecoat was all tore anyway and was way shorter than her dress and ripped at the shoulder and stuffing was coming out and she didn't care. She could ride the bus with me cause her father wasn't home so we held hands and skipped double skips down the road from the bus singing "Around the corner Captain Marvell" till we ran out of breath and couldn't remember the words and laughed and laughed all the way to the back yard where the dirt was hard and we could play little cars after we went in the kitchen where They were drinking iced tea and cooking pintos. I told them this was Gail who used to live next door and had the tiny television where us kids had watched Howdy Doody even if we were too big crowded in front of that little screen where Howdy Doody laughed and we'd laughed back. Now she didn't live here but she could visit cause her father worked late and they told us to go play on the porch where we giggled about how her hair was chopped like boy hair and mine was long and shiny because They scrubbed it so hard every Saturday.

Then Gail left to walk home and They told me never bring her here again did you see that coat two sizes too little and all ripped and dirty and she was smelly like old laundry and they can't help it but don't bring her here. So next day she said hi and I didn't and I didn't look at her again cause she still had on that coat and I knew I couldn't ever talk to her again and I didn't.

Sabrina Jones

Smart Kid in Appalachia

The struggle is real for the smart kid in Appalachia.
Born to the rigid mountains of blue-black collar coalmine country
I cut my teeth within the confines of un-culture
Developing a fractured, sheltered identity
Spawned from the narrow-minded, the bigot...
Ahem.
The honest, hard-working, simple, and proud.
The last generation of a dying tribe trying to firmly ground its roots.
And limbs. And fruits.
My parents say I read too much.
Git ya nose outta that book if you wanna learn sumpin.
But aren't books educational?
Gittin too big for your britches, that's what.
I get scolded for blowing Christmas money on classics.
Be like your sister. Tamagotchi and Z. Cavaricci.
And do her homework. We cain't do no fractions.
Thank God and Satan for the library.
I hoard and hide stories to devour post-bedtime.
Once high school hits, I am too school for cool.
Instead of having curves, I break curves.
Earning evil glares from classmates who don't study,
I learn the southern way – sit down, shut up, play dumb
Miss a question or two, feed the dog my homework, never raise my hand
Scale it back.
Too smart for my own good.
I must avoid being what Plath was – "too dangerously brainy."
So I bury my brain in pop culture, fads, and coal dust.

Still, I can't shake the smarts disease.
I don't marry a coal miner and have a litter of young 'uns after high school (or before).
With the wind to my face, I find my people, find my place.
I go off to "college" (snide snickers – too big for her britches)
And return with degrees to the preacher calling me Dr. Fahrenheit.
I return – to give books as gifts to the limbs and fruits.
An educator and a life-long learner
Who doesn't mind small britches and being too school for cool
If it makes the struggle less real for the smart kid in Appalachia.

Amanda Rodriguez

Sticks and Stones

I wake up on a bouncing school bus to the words "Nigger jew." They laugh as if they've just said something clever. They repeat those words to each other over and over again, "Nigger jew...nigger jew...nigger jew," and I can hear the spit gathered behind their teeth as it hisses. I know they're talking about us.

We learned early on to sit right behind the bus driver to prevent any "incidences," for all the good it does us.

I turn to them, "Hey! Don't say that! I don't ever want to hear you say those words in front of me! Do you understand? *Can* you understand?" I stare at them trying to sound threatening. They shut their mouths and look at me for a second. I turn away and ignore them.

After a little while, I hear them again. They're whispering it now... "nigger jew...fuckin' nigger jews..."

"I said shut the fuck up you goddamned stupid hicks! What the fuck is wrong with you?"

"Hey! Hey! Settle down back there!" How convenient that the bus driver's ears suddenly begin to work. I slam my back into the green, duct-taped seat jarring my sister momentarily from her slumber. Her dark eyes focus briefly on my scowl and then unfocus as she leans her head against the window again.

"Bobby," I say.

I can see purple veins beneath the skin on little Bobby Harris's pale face. He must weigh 90 pounds soaking wet with his redwings on, but that doesn't stop him from talking shit with his stupid little friends.

"What the hell do you want?" His voice is the sound of the country, of coal mines and farms. I hate it.

"Why do you have that Confederate flag on?" He wears it on his blond head like a bandana.

"'Cause I think we never should of gotten rid of them slaves. That's all niggers are good for anyway."

I suppress my instinct to verbally gut him.

"How do you like West Virginia? Don't you like living in West Virginia?"

"Of course."

"Well, then, don't you think it's really disrespectful to wear a Confederate flag? Don't you know that West Virginia seceded from Virginia to stay *with* the Union? That means that West Virginia was against slavery *and* the Confederacy." I had just learned this in our West Virginia History class.

"Huh? What the hell are you talking about?"

I sit on the gym bleachers after my science class ready to go home but having to wait to get on the bus. I hate the bus. I sit at the bottom next to my younger brother, watching the basketball players with disinterest as they warm up for practice. Their shoes squeak on the shiny floor as they run laps. Most of them are skinny with voices that have yet to crack. My little brother sits close to me.

"Hey, wetbacks!" I hear from above me, echoing slightly in the rafters. Jason Peck sits with a group of his friends. Not all of them are young. Some have been held back several years and have grown tall and meaty.

"Shut up!" I hear my own voice echo, and it sounds to me like a small child's plea.

"Why don't you go back to Mexico? Just get back on your boat and go." Laughter. "Or did you guys swim here?" More laughter.

"I'm not Mexican, you fucking idiot!"

"Yeah, I guess she's right. She don't really look Mexican..."

They're right; I don't even have that. Not even that.

"...but your brother over here, now he's definitely

Mexican. Maybe Pablo got at it with your mom, and..."

"We're not Mexican! We're Cuban, stupid!" I look over at my brother, surprised that he has spoken. He is dark and small, even smaller than I feel.

They laugh again. It is more painful now, though, because I know they are laughing at him.

"It's all the same thing. Just get your brown asses back on your boat and go home."

Our oldest sister is not there when we get on the bus. She's supposed to be here. Without her I feel naked and defenseless. I give my brother the window seat, and I take the aisle, hoping to act as a barrier between him and them. Putting on his headset, he stares out the window. He doesn't seem to really look beyond the fingerprints on the glass. I prop my knees up against the seat in front of me. My brand new biology book is a comfort as its thickness rests against my stomach and thighs. Closing my eyes, I pretend to sleep.

Something tickles my cheek, and I open my eyes. Pencil shavings slide off my head, onto my face and lap like snowflakes. Laughter again. I violently brush the top of my head off, and I slap the shavings off my body as if they are poisonous spiders. Bobby Harris's face is only a few inches from mine. His blue eyes mock me. I can see my reflection in his glasses. My face is smudged with lead, but I leave it there. I know he did it. I know it.

"You stupid piece of shit!" I am yelling at him, and he is still smiling, his mouth gaping to reveal all his crooked teeth and the tobacco molded to his gums.

"Hey, now! Young lady, you watch your language on my bus!" The driver glares at me in his long, rectangular mirror. In that mirror, I see grinning faces with eyes fixed on me.

"But he dumped pencil shavings on my head!"

"I did *not*, Bill. I was just doing my homework." He

says it in this sing-song way. He uses that same line all the time. I know that the driver will believe him.

"Just keep it quiet!" His attention goes back to the road.

In a level voice I say, "You better not do anything else." My nails dig into the cover of my textbook until my fingers are white and there are tiny crescent dents in the book's cover.

"Or else what?" Jason Peck in the seat behind me leers. "What you going do, spick?"

His fat fingers reach out and tug at the cord on my brother's headset. I shove his hand away.

"Leave him alone, you fucking Neanderthal!"

"OOOOHHHH!!!" They're all laughing, all around me. "Oh, spick boy can't even take care of hisself! His big sister's gotta take care of him!"

Bobby Harris spits tobacco-colored saliva on my brother's face.

My brother's eyes shift from me to them as he drags the back of his sleeve across his cheek. I know he's afraid because I'm afraid. I can see he resents me for my loudness, for making us targets. In his eyes, though, there is something more than resentment for our tormentors. His hatred is born here. Years of our father didn't do it. A drunk whose philosophy about his children is "out of sight, out of mind," who deserted us for some woman, leaving us nothing of our heritage, not even our language. That anger and hatred waited inside of his small body. It waited for something or someone concrete to focus on. Now I watch as my playful, forgiving brother learns to hate.

In that moment, I think about using my science book to fracture Bobby Harris's skull. I think about the adrenaline rush I will get as I swing the heavy book against his ear. His glasses will be knocked crooked, and he will smack his head on the window with an empty thunk. But I will not stop. I will hit him over and over again as hard as I can for as long as I can. His blood will smear on the window and his teeth will break, but I will keep hitting him. People will remember the whooshing sound my book made as it rushed toward his temple. They will also remember the sound of it connecting with his face and the sound of his jawbones cracking. Someone will have to pull me off him because I won't be able to stop until this feeling in my chest is gone. I think that it will never go away, so I will never stop hitting him. I think, though, that he will never die.

My toes barely brush the gum-stained carpet as I sit at my sister's desk. She and I wait in Mr. Sharp's empty classroom. He and my mother stand in the doorway talking, my mother making graceful hand gestures and Mr. Sharp motionless, his hands behind his back. He is my sister's Social Studies teacher. She paces. I think the routine comforts her, lets her think.

She explains to me that, today, the French teacher came into their class to give a presentation on her trip to Korea. Her trip was wonderful, she reported. The country was beautiful. She said that she didn't understand why America didn't let more Koreans into the country. Koreans are an intelligent, hard-working people, she said. Unlike the Cubans who are "of a lower element," and the U.S. government had let *them* pour into our country. My sister had argued with her unsuccessfully and was sent to the principal's office for her "attitude problem." The principal was the same. "Well, you must admit," he said, "Cubans *are* of a lower element." My sister said that our father proved that untrue. He's an immigrant from Cuba, a lawyer, my sister said, and he graduated at the top of his class in an Ivy League school. "Well," the principal said again, "there are always exceptions."

I feel broken when she tells me she cried. Those people made my sister cry. The strongest, most intelligent person I know had cried because of them.

"I've been hearing a lot of the same sentiment expressed in our faculty meetings," I hear Mr. Sharp's monotone voice say. "They don't want to teach your kids."

My mother has been in a meeting with the idiot principal for hours, and her shoulders slump with exhaustion. "I don't understand."

"They don't want your children in their classes simply because they are Hispanic. Your younger daughter doesn't look very Hispanic." He gestures toward me, and it makes me feel hollow, transparent. "But your other children do. Not only that, but as soon as they read that last name on the roll call, that's it. Your kids don't have a chance."

My mother opens her mouth and closes it. She opens it again. No words come for a while. "But they're good kids. They're bright. They get good grades, and I know they behave in class. I don't understand."

Mr. Sharp just shakes his head.

We understand, though. My sister, brother, and I. We have learned to understand.

Donna Isaac

Summer Job

In the Crystal Mist, the bartender says to pay up or get out,
you go-go booted waitress who wears hot pants to stay cool
who got ripped off by the patron drunk on Windsor and water
who made the little gal drop her tray then stole the wad of ones
that fell like leaf litter onto the crusty carpet in the disco dark
so that she was short and blameworthy though she was guilty
only of working there in the first place since she had an English
degree and couldn't find a job teaching about the Wife of Bath
or the villain Iago or about writing poetry or reading Eliot
but had to slog sloe gin and beer bottles to boys who pinched her ass
and tried to corner her in the walk-in near the meat scraps
or feel her up by the crowded counter or pull down her tube top
while she bent to retrieve the dropped quarter she needed to pay up
or get fired from a job she had to have to pay off student loans
to get free from her mother's suburban split level to pay for the books
that spilled from cardboard boxes and filled makeshift bookshelves
next to LPs by Foreigner, Rod Stewart, the Bee Gee's, the Stones
or pay for that bag of weed surreptitiously stashed
inside a mitten her grandmother had knitted with nubby yarn
the one stuffed inside the pocket of her dead father's coat
that also held a stick of stale Juicy Fruit and a washer for a leaky faucet
and another quarter that she saved up to rub together
with the one she eventually retrieves from the sticky floor
by the wastebasket brimming with plastic cups and swizzle sticks
and little umbrellas that open and shut on her life
as she defends herself from the accusation of theft
since it was the drunk who ripped her off in the first place
so she finally throws down the bar rag spins the tray
like a Frisbee into the boss man's chest and says that she quits
can't take this bullshit anymore and turns to split
the milling crowd like Moses did the Red Sea
only the inebriated girl with the earrings like golden hula hoops

doesn't get the message leans in and barfs on her white boots
adding indignity to an already ignominious exit while the dancers
keep on dancing unaware of the drama and spinning around
and around like the dreams in their heads and the music
follows her out the door into the parking lot dotted with arc lamps
surrounded by desperate moths and she still hears
Donna Summer as she pulls out into the night
out of the Mist into the awaiting rest of her life, singing,
"Enough is enough is enough I can't go on I can't go on no more no."

Alicia Wright

For You in Case You've Forgotten

I want to tell you that your parents have not fixed
the garage window that shattered when the ball
you kicked at my head in the dark swung wild
the night we didn't speak—

the night before we were caught scrambling
on hands and knees across the lawn in dim
pre-dawn, gathering our empties before
your father left for work.

Your sister remembers the apples we threw
from the hilltop at cars on the highway below,
gone soft but still green, and the pickup that slid
to a loud stop across the faded center line;

you should know that the snack-bar has closed,
its parking lot studded now by overflow
from the new video-gambling café next door;

that a Jehovah's Witness cornered me today,
read to me from Psalms and I cannot believe
in God. It has been raining for days.

Willie Davis

A Subdivision of Heaven

As a child, Roxy-Jane Leckett preached to the chickens in the garbage heap that separated her property line from her neighbor's yard. Her mother was a constant runaway, and her father loved chasing, so Roxy was reared by a cousin who lived three counties away, but who drove into town on the weekends to check on her.

The family never threw anything away. It added to the sadness of the world, Roxy told us, all of the discard, how quickly we say goodbye. On a practical level, it meant piles of garbage cluttered up their house and enormous yard.

When her mother tried her hand at homesteading, instead of planting a proper garden, she spread the seed haphazardly around the backyard. The chickens were a leftover from a season the parents decided to raise their own eggs. The neighborhood children loved feeding them, so when a fox or stray cat would turn the coop into a mess of blood and feathers, some kindly neighbor would bring a replacement White Leghorn to pacify the kids. The cats came for the chickens and the dogs came for the cats and the rats came for the garbage and us kids came for the show. We called the house "The Ark" for the endless parade of animals, but also because every evening, Roxy, starting from age eleven, stood on her porch, holding a Bible she never opened, and spoke the good word to all of us.

Roxy was a natural preacher, passing judgment before she was old enough for pimples. We would gather to watch her bless the chickens, each sentence sounding high and light as a song. "Ain't no shame in sinning," she said to a brown guinea hen. "The shame is in living a life unexamined."

When we were young, not all of us were allowed at the Leckett House. Through the unending game of telephone that kids play with their families, some of the chickens or opossums sniffing the trash turned into wolves or cottonmouths. My brother swore he found himself face to face with an AIDS-monkey on the porch. Nobody believed him, but a few of us boys carried sharpened sticks to protect ourselves and show off for Roxy and the neighborhood girls.

Every summer, the Leckett parents dropped off their daughter at a religious camp in Knott County. "Spiritual stamping grounds" is what Roxy called it, a phrase she purloined from a camp counselor. She made it sound fun—more canoeing and pick-up basketball than fire and brimstone and blowing your priest—but I knew not to ask my mom if I could go with her. For one, it wasn't Christianity exactly, but a hippie Christian offshoot. The long-haired preachers insisted we were already dead, all of us, and currently occupying heaven. "What do we know of heaven?" Roxy asked the animals one morning. "We got rewarded with life forever. But we're living now, ain't we? We have our heaven without the pain of dying. I've won, and you've won, and we've all won, my friends—now we need to learn how to stop playing."

The other reason I could never go with Roxy to Knott County was that whenever she came home from camp—starting at the age of twelve—she brought back enough industrial strength acid to keep the neighborhood children tripping until All Saints Day. Roxy called it eyeglasses for the spirit, a chance for the soul to step out of the skin. For her, acid was a decoder ring to see all the invisible ink God had spilled before us.

We got older. My mother went off to be with God, if you're of the denomination that believes God lives in a pinewood coffin in Lexington's poor folks cemetery. Roxy and I fell in love with each other, though not at the same time. We pretended our love didn't matter, but that's like walking away mid-face tattoo and acting as though it won't hurt your campaign.

My brother teased me endlessly. "That girl smells like a hobo's ballbag, and her adult teeth are going to last about as long as her baby teeth did." He called her "Kentucky Fried

Christian" and "Mary Magda-hen," and I kept failing to make him sorry.

In matters of the heart, I am a vandal, but I couldn't smartass my way out of Roxy's charm. After years of study and emulation, I counted myself among the devoted animals lining the edges of the Leckett yard.

"It takes no mind to be scared," Roxy told me once when I called her after midnight. "The best part about the good news is that it has you whether you want it or not." It was hard not to catch the believer-bug. We owed each other our faith.

There were horse farms just outside of town where the grass turned yellow in the summer and brown in the fall, and you could stand on one end and see the horizon before you see the property line. The horses live with more room and more freedom than almost any human could imagine. Their world was the space in front of them, and so their world always changed. As a result, they were faster and stronger than us. All of nature bowed at their hooves.

One day, many years later, Roxy herself became a missing person. At that point, she had renamed herself Alexis Rock, unwilling to take her new husband's name but also unwilling to leave her name unchanged. She left behind a husband and a daughter, and took with her a baby on the way who the doctors predicted would be large and restless. The police said there was no evidence of foul play, thereby maintaining the police's perfect record when it came to being helpful in my life. The rest of us searched for her, but only when we grew sick of mourning.

I'll remember her touch long after her words have run together. I'll remember the fresh chill of disappointment when that touch went away, how it hit me like air rushing into my stomach when my car takes a hill too fast and loses contact with the road. She will be the last figure I see before I die— she'll be the pennies on my eyes. It'll feel as it does every night before sleep, almost real and almost enough.

My brother was our cynic. He lives his life in the vegetable world. What didn't press back against his fingertips was unreal. Roxy is our believer. Dreams were reality to her, the difference no more substantial than the difference between soup and stew.

I come from the meantime, the in-between. My friends say I lack conviction, but it's just that I'm doomed to live in the middle-management of beliefs. My life is now and will forever remain fully haunted by halfway ghosts.

Leslie Clark

Driving in the Dark

The nighthawks left weeks ago, traveling
at night, stopping only to swirl around gas station lights,
feed, then resume their journey.
Traveling by night is a gift to savor.

Every summer we would drive back to West Virginia.
The last miles ended in the dark,
road unraveling through mountains,
the scent of cool air,

the clicking sound of the silver button
on the floorboard that turned the brights on and off.
Headlights cut stripes through the fog.
Car windows rolled down, skin soaking up the wind.

Driving home, cresting a hill between trees
swaying in the blackness. At the road's edge,
irregular pieces of moon
are tacked onto a galvanized rail.

Kris Gillis

Beer Delivery

The hollowed out fifteen-passenger van
holds a hundred cases of beer
but today I've only got about forty
and I'm weaving through Wolfe County, Kentucky
in this van emblazoned with a Heineken logo
but nobody out here drinks Heineken
it's all Milwaukee's Best or Best Light
or if you've got money "regular Miller"
which is what Carroll calls Miller Lite,
Carroll who is off on the main roads in the side-loader
while I run all the odd stops – his words –
which I love because the roads that give
his big truck so much trouble – "turns so sharp
you could turn your head and kiss your butt" –
is what my granddad or my great granddad
or maybe just my dad by way of one of them always said –
are a breeze in the van,
                                        and the romance of cruising alone
on back roads loaded down with beer
for bars that are nothing but a double-wide or a barn
outfitted with refrigerators and high stools
in the middle of a corn field or down in a holler
is almost too much,
                                        so I'm running with the AC off
and the windows down, hanging my elbow out,
and flicking ash from my Doral cigarette –
Carroll's brand but I smoke them in the summer
when I'm out in this van with all these stacks of beer
on these back roads – a trade up from the usual stacks
of books and dirty dorm hallways,
                                                    when I crest

that big hill and the trees all clear out
and I put it in park just for a minute
because Carroll's old and has over fifteen hundred cases
and will move them all if I let him, but I won't let him,
which is why I'm out here in the first place
because they trust me to take care of him for his old lady,
but still, I stop.
                    I look out over rolling green hills
and tobacco plants and dirt paths worn into the smooth slopes
and I listen to the low growl of the diesel engine and the hum
of the cicadas and the distant lowing of the cattle,
and I take just a minute and sit.

Richard Hague

Hoopies, Hillbillies, & Me

Adapted from The 2014 Hughes Lecture,
West Liberty University, West Liberty, WV

March 9, 1965. I was a seventeen year-old senior at Steubenville Catholic Central High School, just about 20 miles upriver, and at some point that day—I know not the exact hour—I became a hillbilly. As a matter of fact, all up and down the Ohio Valley, in places like Toronto, Ohio, and Mingo Junction, Rayland and Empire and Alikanna, in George's Run and Pottery Addition and Shadyside and Brilliant and Bridgeport and Empire—all at once, as if in some sort of unaccountable "Foggy Mountain Breakdown"-accompanied Rapture, *everyone* in those eastern-and-southern-most Ohio counties became a hillbilly.

Perhaps it happened during my English class, conducted by Sr. Mary Doris, a young Dominican nun who was to leave the order soon, in those turbulent and revolutionary Sixties, and then marry, have three children, divorce, at last to discover herself a lesbian and take a partner she still has, all the while working as a Jungian psychoanalyst in New York City. What a long journey from teaching Johnny Sobolewski and Pat Madden and Sharon Kocal and Kathy Hudak in that Appalachian mill town—in one way—in another, how oddly parallel the events—the diversity of Steubenville's ethnic and cultural mix converging somehow with the dizzying variety and cosmopolitan complexes, neuroses, and re-inventions of New York City.

In just the Catholic community of Steubenville, for example, there were several parishes that fed into the central high school, many of them relatively ethnically undiluted. Many people, ininformed about the complexity of the region, assume that all Appalachians are alike, Scotch-Irish in origin, all sharing the same foods and folkways and music. Definitely not so. For example, my parish, St. Peter's, was Irish Catholic, mostly, populated by Carrigs, McDonoughs, Cavanaughs, Kirkpatricks, Doyles, Joyces, and McCulloughs. Not far away, there was St. Stanislaus School, the Polish parish, whose kids were named Mieczkowsi, Stasuleiwicz, Kalinkiewicz, Kuzikowski. Not far from them was St. Anthony's, the Italian parish, whose students bore names like Antonucci, Di Benedetto, DeFederico, Carinci, and Ciancetta—Tommy Ciancetta, by the way, was my close friend, music group mate, and a graduate of West Liberty State Teacher's College (this university's former name) in 1969, where he played on the football team.

My life-long interest in names was launched in those days, and the diversity of ethnic backgrounds they reflected has helped me realize the complexity of Appalachian culture to a degree people from more homogeneously Scotch-Irish regions of Southern and Central Appalachia might not. A hillbilly, I learned early on, could be someone like Mike Swartz, a Czechoslovakian Jew and father of my best friend Roger, whose wife was an Englishwoman named Ada. Mike did a lot of so-called hillbilly things: he collected, dried, and sold ginseng. (This, of course, implies that he knew the woods intimately; to find ginseng in that industrialized colony of railroads, coal mines, coke factories, power plants, and steel mills was an accomplishment, in natural history terms, equivalent to a state championship in football, to mention what was really valued there.) He taught us boys how to catch hellgrammites, a good fish bait. Every year, he sold his harvest of coonskins—two dollars for a regular, three dollars for a mostly-black one. Over the hill from their backyard, he kept the bluetick and redbone hounds he hunted with. At the same time as he engaged in these sorts of woodscrafts, he operated a high-tech crane in the mill and toted home what was probably a pretty handsome paycheck weekly.

Or a hillbilly, I learned, could be—*could be*—someone like Steven Hart, a friend of the family's who was Steubenville's health inspector and pathologist. He knew I was interested in science and natural history (around that time I received a scholarship from the Steubenville Audubon Club and traveled down to nearby Oglebay Park for a week-long Nature Camp). One day, after my parents' intervention, Mr. Hart invited me to his lab, where he showed me slides of smallpox and plague and cholera.

Or a hillbilly, I learned, could be—*could be*— and I'll clarify this *could be* business in a minute—a hillbilly could be my own grandmother, Helen Madigan Hague, and each of her four rosary-toting sisters, only one of whom ever married, the other three living together for almost ninety years of work as, variously, an official of the Steubenville draft board (that was Aunt Miriam), nurse in the Tin Mill of Weirton Steel (that was Aunt Dorothy) and permanent housekeeper for them all (that was Aunt Leona, aka Nonie.) All of them became—or had the chance to become— hillbillies at the same time I did. And therefore, all the details of their lives, all the details of life in Steubenville during the height of its economic and industrial power, all the details of their Catholic culture of rosaries and Adoration of the Eucharist and Stations of the Cross…these were all a part of what it could mean and still could mean to be a hillbilly, at least from this neck of the woods. No snake handlers, no shape-note singers, no moonshiners. Well—at least not that I knew of. Come to think of it, though, my dad could still score a pint of white whenever he wanted to, and it sat next to his Scotch and his Irish whiskey in the liquor cabinet. Just as going to synagogue was part of what it could mean to be a hillbilly in Steubenville, or studying philsophy at the College of Steubenville, or reading about Dutch Elm Disease in the Carnegie Library while sitting beneath a portait of Andrew Carnegie, who made war against an array of ethnically-diverse proto-hillbillies during the Homestead Steel Strike of 1892—

this too was part of what it *could* mean and *could continue* to mean, to be a hillbilly.

The occasion of our possibly becoming hillbillies—a term we never used in Steubenville, incidentally—I will come back to this in a moment, also—the occasion was the creation of the Appalachian Regional Commission. John F. Kennedy, disturbed by the poverty he witnessed here in West Virginia during his campaign, established the President's Appalachian Regional Commission in the year he died, 1963. That led to the law, signed later by Lyndon Johnson, by which the Appalachian Region was defined in the terms set by the federal government. Because of this, on Valentine's Day of 1965, I was roughly a Midwesterner; by St. Patrick's Day, I was, officially, an Appalachian.

I use the term Appalachian now in place of hillbilly. Actually, as I have said, in the Steubenville of my boyhood and youth, the term hillbilly was rarely used. When we looked across the river from Steubenville to West Virginia, oblivious to the fact that we were destined to become, in the eyes of the law, the same thing as them, the word that came to our lips was "hoopy." Anyone with a West Virginia license plate in downtown was derided as a 'hoopy" and was expected to do something dumb in the driving department. My acquaintance Tim Russell, a poet born in Steubenville, who worked for Weirton Steel (and a student at West Liberty Teacher's College back in the day), once offered a theory on the origin of "hoopy" to me. He said it referred to anyone from the area around Wheeling, where workers now settled in Weirton, say, might return by "going down hoopy"—meaning to the place where barrel hoops were made in the 19th century.

So "hoopy," referring to individuals or the region they're from—both perhaps—sounds as plausible as the similar explanation you can find in the online *Urban Dictionary*. Whatever, "hoopy" was what we said in Steubenville in place of "hillbilly."

On the day I abruptly found myself living in what the government now said was Appalachia (it was a Tuesday), I would have left for school at around 7 in the morning, having to walk down our long, switchbacked hill to Lincoln Avenue, where I would catch the bus to the West End of Steubenville, the site of the relatively new Catholic Central High School. At the time, I was dating a girl with the deliriously melodious name of Desolina Casini. Previously, I had dated Khristine Eroshevich, a smart scholar who had won two National Science Foundation grants to do research at Woods Hole, Massachusetts during her high school summers. After moving to California shortly after medical school at The Ohio State University, she eventually got mixed up with the actress and former Playmate of the Year Anna Nicole Smith, and, after acting as Smith's psychiatrist, had her medical license suspended as a result of Smith's death by an overdose of drugs Khristine prescribed for her. Khristine and Desolina too, despite the exotica of Bevery Hills infamy and the ethnicity of Italian-American Steubenville were, and remain, by birthplace and government decree, hillbillies.

But wait a minute: a hillbilly, according to the stereotype, is a shiftless, ignorant, white, cabin-dwelling inbreed with bad teeth and a taste for corn likker, right? How in the hell does a graduate of the Ohio State University Medical School, and a long-practicing celebrity psychiatrist, living most of her life in California, qualify as a hillbilly? How does a sweet Italian-American girl, the cousin of Tito Carinci, one of Steubenville's most notorious Mafia gangsters, fit the received notion? Are you kidding me? That's exactly the question most people in Steubenville would have asked on March 9th, 1965, had there been some general announcement of our universal metamorphosis: Me, a hillbilly? Are you serious?

Well, the wonder of it is that all the people, mostly women, who came into Junedale Meat Market from 1961-1965, the years I worked weekdays and Saturdays there in downtown Steubenville—they were possibly hillbillies now. It's a remarkable thing to digest: the dark-haired second-generation Serbian women with vivid lips? Hillbillies. Those rotund Italian women still speaking their native language and shouting to me Basta! Basta! if I gave them too much ground beef? Hillbillies. The Greeks and Lithuanians and Slovaks and Hungarians, the African American women who lugged home their frosty ten-pound frozen buckets of chittlins, or the Sicilian women who carried out balls of string-tied provolone and packages of prosciutto and salami—all hillbillies. The priests, rabbis, nuns, ministers—hillbillies, all of them.

Now: lest you think that I am making fun of this whole idea—of becoming a hillbilly—of becoming an Appalachian—consider this: given all the hours and effort I have spent since then, studying, writing, learning, teaching, wandering through and being taught about Appalachia, and hanging around with other Appalachians from all over the region—that day, March 9, 1965, was as important a day in my life as a writer and person as was the day I enrolled in college, or the day I married. It changed everything, even as I kept on trucking, mostly oblivious to the vast possibilites and realities of a world that would unfold before me for the rest of my life. The day I became a hillbilly—and by now I hope you see that I am deliberately beating the term to death, in hopes that it, and the myopic stereotypes it conveys, will cease to exist except for pointed literary effect, or tribal identification—I began to enter all the obvious complexity of the population, history, culture, and the soon-to-be-expanding literary canon of Appalachia. I had found a homeplace of historical, linguistic, economic, political, and literary significance. I no longer lived in what sophomoric wits everywhere would call "Stupidville;" I now lived in a place of great interest and history, and of course (since my home town was certainly a part of what the novelist, activist and the year 2000 candidate for Governor of West Virginia Denise Giardina has rightly characterized as a colony of industrial capitalism) a place of great suffering and of environmental degradation.

This was a choice on my part. The naming of the region by the federal government for various administrative purposes did not, obviously, make hillbillies out of those Italian and Serbian and African American women I served at Junedale Meat Market. I am sure they would have felt much closer ties to their national and ethnic origins than they would have to the notion of hillbilly or hoopy or even Appalachian. Herein lies the fascination of the whole story as I have come to learn it: Appalachian-ness may well be something a person may not only be born into, but a way of being and acting that can be chosen, consciously cultivated, taken pride in, I think. At least in my case, this is true. And if you don't come to such consciousness, perhaps, even though you grew up in Bluefield, West Virginia, as Giardina did, and as Homer Hickham, chief of "The Rocket Boys" of *October Sky* fame and a previous speaker in this series did, a person may nevertheless reject any and all of the baggage that comes along with the idea of hillbilly, hoopy, or even "Appalachian." (Neither Giardina nor Hickham reject their roots.)

I think I was predisposed to accept my Appalachianness by several factors. Five generations of my family lived in Steubenville, and for all that time, as far as I know, in or around one small neighborhood called "The Patch." This kind of placedness, this kind of staying put and (its forced inverse, the bemoaning of displacement, of not being "down hoopy") is traditionally an Appalachian habit, and that it is no longer only makes it clear, by dint of literature and music, how much Appalachians miss "down home" when we're uprooted. Secondly, though I am technically an urban Appalachian, my interest in the natural world was fed deeply by the fact that I wandered the hollows and ridges, ponds and creeks of the outlying precints of Steubenville freely, and at great length. Thirdly was my father's purchase of fifteen acres in rural Monroe County,

Ohio, and my eventual rustication there for whole summers in my early manhood. Being in close contact with able storytellers, like Jim Winland, originally from Martins Ferry, just across the river from here, and with bobcats, copperheads, greenbrier thickets, whippoorwills, coal miners, and country storekeeps deepened my sense of place and culture.

Several other formative experiences resulted from my part of the world becoming a part of Appalachia. A few years after that spring of 1965, I was granted the privilege of submitting for my Master's Thesis at Xavier University a collection of poems based on the history of Steubenville, going all the way back to Indian days and coming up to the then-present place. In an intellectual revelation akin to the one for the character in Moliere's *Le Bourgeois Gentilhomme*, who realized that he had been speaking prose all his life, I began to realize I'd been Appalachian all my life without knowing it. I began to re-orient my mind and my knowledge to this new perspective on where I was in the world and where I fit in the Appalachian and indeed in the larger American experience.

Equally formative was my attending the Appalachian Writers Workshop in Hindman, Kentucky, starting one summer in the late Seventies. I'd learned about it from my friend and former college roommate, the writer and activist Mike Henson, whose novels *Ransack* and *Tommy Perdue* and book of stories *Small Room with Trouble on My Mind* chronicle the hard times of dislocated Appalachians, also known as SAMs—Southern Appalachian Migrants—in Cincinnati's Over-The-Rhine and elsewhere in southern Ohio. (His latest book, a prize-winning collection entitled *The Way The World Is: The Maggie Boylan Stories*, is a brilliant and painful look at addiction in the Appalachian counties of Ohio.) Mike was the first to tell me told me about a meeting of Appalachian writers that I might be interested in attending.

I went down to Hindman, deep in the mountains of eastern Kentucky, with lots of uncertainty, not only about my own credentials as an Appalachian writer, but about the place itself. For example, I knew that Knott County was pretty remote, and that it was, in terms of alcohol, dry. In my type-A need to have things under control, I went down a day early, just in case I got lost on the way. I took a room in the Hindman Hotel, a tiny building next to the courthouse, on whose steps, I was to learn later, at least one murder by shooting had occurred. The manager's little desk was just outside the door of my room, so when, after arriving, I got thirsty for a beer, I was so paranoid that I took the can out of the cooler I'd smuggled in, covered it with my pillow, as if I were going to smother it, and popped the tab under there so it couldn't be heard. Even then, for all my sweating caution, I had visions of the local constabulary busting the door down and hauling me off to some rickety jailhouse down some lonesome holler where the sun refused to shine. It was the most nervous beer I'd ever drunk in my life.

The next day I made my way two blocks down the street, crossed the bridge over the Forks of Troublesome Creek, to the campus of Hindman Settlement School, and registered. Within a couple of hours, I was sitting in the same room with James Still, Cratis Williams, Harriet Arnow, Gurney Norman, Shirley Williams, Jim Wayne Miller, whose archetypal modern Appalachian poems include *Brier: His Book*, "brier" being yet another terms for "hillbilly" or hoopy" or SAM or Appalachian, and Albert Stewart, the founder of *Appalachian Heritage* magazine and the workshop, as well as thirty or forty other writers from all around. In terms of Appalachian culture, it was like suddenly finding myself in a room with, and having leisurely conversational access to, the equivalents of William Faulkner, W.E.B. DuBois, Ralph Waldo Emerson, Johnny Appleseed, Mike Fink, Isadora Duncan, Mother Jones, and Ralph Stanley. I knew only the slightest bits of the work and power of those Appalachian scholars and writers and artists before that day; by the end of the week, I was giddy with the new knowledge and the new mentors life had presented me.

Not to mention my fellow mere mortals and participants: one was Anne Campbell, at the time the Appalachian librarian at UK. Another was Jerry Wayne Williamson, editor of *Appalachian Journal*, and later author of the Weatherford Award-winning *Hillbillyland: What The Movies Did To The Mountains and What the Mountnains Did To The Movies*. I think too Jim "Ski King" Webb was there, now the author of what Gurney Norman claims "belongs on any list of the greatest one hundred poems of all time." That poem would be the title work of his collected poems, *Get In, Jesus*, which everyone should know and read annually, maybe on March 9. And there was Danny Miller, later a long-time professor of Appalachian Studies and eventually head of the Literature and Language Department at Northern Kentucky University, as well as dozens of other aspiring or already-accomplished Appalachian writers and activists.

The week there altered my cultural DNA; I was to return for almost every year for a couple of decades, celebrating many of my birthdays there in the first week of August. I was to take part in back-porch tall-tale fests with Jim Wayne Miller, whose generous mentoring of me and many others went on for years. There, too, I was to instigate the First Annual Troublesome Creek Olympics, one major event of which was the Cross Troublesome Creek Chair Toss, conspiring with Jerry Wayne and my friends Jim Quinlivan and Bob Collins. I was to swap tales with Cratis Williams, author of the seminal and monumental *The Southern Mountaineer in Fact and Fiction*, whose knowledge of Appalachian literature, culture, and folklore was literally encyclopedic, and whose often bawdy humor was a swarper's delight.

In the long run, perhaps the most important event in those days subsequent to the Appalachian Writers Workshop was my joining up with the Southern Appalachian Writers Cooperative. Originally formed in the mid-70s by writers and political activists, SAWC had gone partially dormant until later in the decade, when it resurrected during some pretty heady years of what some have called the Appalachian Renaissance—the same ground-force that fought, successfully, the Broad Form Deed, that fueled the multiple runs for West Virginia governor of SAWC member Bob Henry Baber, and that prepared the ground for the first Appalachian Writers Workshop. I rode down to Highlander Center in New Market, Tennnesse, where SAWC had first come into being, with some other friends in Gurney Norman's Volkswagen van with visions of Divine Right's trip dancing in my head. I'll not forget the writing prompt Gurney led that resulted in tears as several participants touched tender and wounded places with their words. Memorably, both Jim Wayne and Gurney cavorted at subsequent meetings on the hillsides of Highlander wearing various cheap electronic devices—neon-green glowing googly eyes, plastic rings with little lights in place of their jewels—that had been given out by the ever-hustling and joking Ski King Webb—born, by the way, in Shadyside, Ohio, just across the river and down a bit from West Liberty. A brief pome of his captures something of his literary trickster's and out-of-the-wilderness prophet's personality and voice:

Original Sin

I believe in
  Original Sin

It's just hard
  to think of
    something new

So this is just the beginning of an ever-growing cast of Appalachian characters and writers I bcame part of for going on forty years.

Before SAWC, I may have been Appalachian, but after it, I became much more politically aware and, in company of like-minded activists and writers, found more of a public voice and shared mission as a writer than I had ever had before.

To summarize, then, the important milestones in my still-evolving understanding of what it means to me to be a hillbilly:

—The formation of the Appalachian Regional Commision, which at least in some legal and formal way, decalred me an Appalachian,

—Many years of continuing attendance and sometimes teaching at the Appalachian Writers Workshop in Hindman,

—Joining and serving occasionally as co-coordinator of The Southern Appalachian Writers Cooperative, as well as editing its literary journal *Pine Mountain Sand & Gravel,* and,

—Finally, coming to learn the Highlander Center's connection to civil rights (there is for example, a photograph of Martin Luther King, Jr., Pete Seeger, Rosa Parks, and Ralph Abernathy standing in front of the Highlander Center's library, taken in 1957), its connection to social justice, and its importance in not only mountain politics, but national politics, and finally, coming to understandthat activism can take many forms, including creative writing.

All of these contributed to the somewhat herky-jerky but usually-forwarding literary, cultural, and political education of this particular Northern Appalachian. For all of it, I count myself blessed and lucky. It has, in great part, shaped my adult life as a citizen and writer, and has accounted for some of my deepest satisfactions.

So I'd like to end with a poem written in gratitude, after one of my early weekends at Highlander with SAWC. Originally published in *Appalachian Journal,* I hope it captures the spirit of the organization and its people, themselves inseparable from my own Appalachian-ness:

Talking Together

Annual meeting of the Southern Appalachian Writers Cooperative, Highlander Center, Tennessee, l982

Lord, how our voices often mingle,
creeks rounding down from a thousand miles
to wed the same bright river

And how we mouth our favorite names:
say *poplar, sycamore, broom sedge*
like prayers

And how we have seen the same birds
flock among the white pine groves
of the oldground we've helped heal,

And how we seem to have found the same stories,
seen the same men on street corners
of small towns so barren
thay have no football team

And how we have loved women who look and speak like sisters
And how we have hunted the same deer
on stands decades apart,
And how we have found the same stones in creeks

And how we have seen the same wonders at night
in places hundreds of miles distant
(wild cherry branches shuttling in the breeze,
Arcturus living like an eye above the oak)

And how we have failed the same jobs,
workers slumped over Chevys and Fords,
machinists hurt in our hearts by slivers of steel,
hunters limping upridge with bloodied feet

And how, when we find outselves together,
standing around gas pumps or stoves in old stores,
waiting for tires to be changed,
for children to be drilled by the clinic dentist in town,
for fathers to die in the hospitals of county seats,

We find something to say that meant us,
that names us neighbors and kin,
that finds within us words to connect:
coon hounds loved in common,
a relative with the same name,
a character true to type in all our places:

Lord, how our lives often mingle,
how we mouth our favorite names,
how we sing in voices old, flat, or sweet:

How we know we know one another,
how we love even what we hate
for how it brings us together.

Thomas Alan Holmes

Throwing Down in Vinemont

I had broken the cast metal door handle
from the driver's door of my old Pontiac,
taken the one from the seat right behind me,
thinking I never had passengers back there,
and driven to Vinemont to pick up a cousin
who later would melt sealed his eyelids
when as an adult he could not keep
from using the meth he was cooking
to supplement money he'd gotten from pawning
the jewelry from B&Es from Morgan
and Madison Counties. I think it was leverage,
not that I'm one likely to snap metal pieces
apart, but my elbow, positioned just right,
let my fingers flex, curling inside
the curved handle to pop it. Front windows down,
down the new 31 towards Hartselle, I saw him,
looking sick by the flea market huddled
in Lacon, dressed in a down-layered jacket
too warm for midsummer, red trucker's cap
pulled so hard down his head that his hair
stuck out like its own brim. This was in '77,
and I'd just graduated from high school,
about six weeks away from a dorm room,
and he must have been about twelve,
his dad moved out almost a year,
and his mom on her third boyfriend since.
I had known she was crazy for years,
but I thought her first husband could stand it
until he moved out and she drifted much quicker
than we could account for, a family wanting
to help but cast off like a life that can no longer fit.

So I picked the kid up, thinking he'd climb
inside and take shotgun, but he jumped
straight into the backseat, rolling down
both the windows and lying still, all
out of sight of my mirror and singing
along with the radio crap I hardly
remember, since that car had only AM.
Nearly eighty, the wind through the windows
was parching, and my car was roaring
the way I think fighter jets roar, running
smooth down the highway, due south
towards Vinemont, as I headed home.
Near the big water tower, just two miles
above the last drive-in in Cullman,
next door to the trailer park where he was living
with his crazy mother and boyfriend *du jour*,
I saw a red flash in the mirror and heard
a loud yell from my cousin, the kid in the back
I've not named, because if he should learn
about what I'm writing, he might realize
it's a lie and then stir up his mother,
whose current addiction has led to her making
some death threats to people I know.
So the kid starts to yell, I pull off to the shoulder,
and he tries to climb out of the car,
but the door on the side has no handle, and he
starts in kicking the other door, acting a fool,
because he could get out on that side if he
just had the presence of mind to slide over,
and I'm getting fired up because it's my own car
that he's scuffing up, kicking the door panel
in his broken down "Earth shoes"—I swear it—
and all that I want to do then is to reach
through the window, grab his bare ankle,

and yank the small clown out the back,
but I grab him and snap his leg just like
the handle, and then, bloody murder, he got
that much louder, but I saw his cap
in the road, ran to fetch it, and threw
it back into the car, telling him that he broke
like a wishbone, that I'd drive to the ER
if he'd just be quiet, that he was a brittle
broke kid. And now he's seared blind,
just a mid-forties meth head, and I could count
all of the things I have broken by accident
since that day on my left hand.

Steven Paul Lansky

Jesus and the Big Tree

Jesus lived in California when he was a teenager.
He settled in Palo Alto under a redwood tree
among the hippie transplants from Kentucky.
He sowed wild oats, dug a garden,
collected worms, traded in seeds, hung tie-dyed
curtains, printed lettering on T-shirts for children
with iron-on technology, kept rabbits
after learning about the Magic Rabbit from Gurney,
square danced at local elementary schools,
lived beyond His means, joined the Briarpatch Grocery,
had his black three-speed bicycle—recovered
from the town dump—run over in the Grocery parking lot,
left normal life for Californication and
never returned to the Jewish culture.

When the Pranksters left Palo Alto to cash in on the real estate,
He relocated to East Palo Alto. He loved
the dirt streets down from Whiskey Gulch,
wooden fences, fig trees, and an outdoor dining
area under a wisteria arbor, plus the fact that
the property had been neglected by Amazons.

This was before dotcoms, before internet, before
Reagan, but when the Buddhists were well-entrenched.
It's rumored that Jesus met Arjuna, the questioner,
and they leapt off roof-tops together,
sat in hot tubs, cavorted on Pescadero beach,
cared for the blind by riding with them on tandem
bicycles. Jesus picked up a few musical instruments
in those early years. One night riding in Gurney's
blue Karmann Ghia, after swapping stories
for hours at Foothill Junior College, Gurney advised

Jesus that the mistakes He made
wouldn't count until He turned thirty.
It was this kind of thinking that led to Jesus'
resurrection and things of that nature.

Cody S. Decker

A Pinky's Worth of Character

When I'm out and about
I make it a point
To not
Make a fool of myself
I tend to always have control
Of what I say and what I do
Even if I've had a few
So when I meander
Among the crowds
Trying to find
The smoking section
I always keep it in mind
To keep my pinky on the bottom
Of the glass as I hold it
A small but strong assurance
Because if my pinky is there
The glass won't fall
And I won't waste the money
I spent on my drink
And I won't catch the glares
From those who still have
A firm grasp
On theirs
And that's good
Because nothing says
Fool
Like dropping your drink
On your way to the door

Mindy Dawn Silvergarden

The Tavern

As Katie O'Halloran found herself lying on her belly, sandwiched between the last shelf and the hardwood floor, she thanked God for her father's tendency to leave projects unfinished. As long as it looked acceptable from the front where the customers could see, it was good enough for Dutch O'Halloran. Just the previous autumn she helped him build the shelves behind the bar and install the trim around the dining room, working on the renovation along with Dutch and his brothers. He inherited the tavern from his grandfather nearly ten years earlier, just before Katie turned three. Had he bothered to finish all the cabinetry behind the bar of the family tavern, she'd have nowhere to hide from the flying bullets or the shouting, cursing men.

That Tuesday afternoon had started out like most any other. Band and choir practice after school, followed by a noisy bus ride home into the township. At the intersection of Conemaugh Road and Old Pike road she departed the bus and crossed the street into the tavern where she immediately began the chores of cleaning the dining room and checking the napkin & straws, ice and cups and so on. She was allowed to look and count the bottles, but had to leave a note about what needed what. Once, the tavern got a fine from liquor control because someone saw her carrying a few bottles of booze from storage into the bar. Now, all she could do was baby work. Napkins and straws—sheesh! Any lame-brain could do that. She was pretty sure it was nasty old Mrs. Lenewski that told on her. So now, she made sure that anytime she ran into old Mrs. Lenewski, she'd smile, but in her mind she'd be thinking, "Eff you, nasty old Mrs. Lenewski who thinks I'm a baby! Eff you!" Katie really wanted to say it out loud, but if anyone ever caught wind of it, so would Mama and Katie'd be in trouble for a very long time. If she was allowed to do real work, she might not have been in the tavern's tap room when the men showed up.

Now she was wondering how long these shouting, cursing men would be in trouble for. If it was up to her, they'd be in trouble forever, messing up the dining room she just cleaned. But what about sweet old Mr. Gordon? He had been sitting in the back section of the dining room, reading the paper and drinking coffee like every Tuesday and Thursday since she could remember. He was like part of the family, making himself at home and starting a pot of coffee at the waitress station on his own when he came in, before the dining room was actually opened. She hoped he'd heard the noise and left through the side doors. She thought about Mr. Gordon getting hurt and those men. Maybe old Mrs. Lenewski was right—maybe she was just a baby after all. There was nothing she could do for Mr. Gordon.

The shouting, cursing, shooting men were going on about money and a horse and a mustache. She could hear Uncle Tommy's voice, too, but didn't understand. Uncle Tommy didn't have any horses or a mustache. If the gift of cheap hair barrettes he gave her for her birthday a few weeks earlier was any indication, he didn't have any money, either. The closest thing anyone had to horses was motorcycles. Some of the guys who came to the tavern had mustaches, but what did that have to do with anything? Katie was thinking about this when she heard a pop and felt a thud on the other side of the bar from where she was hiding. She turned her head to peer out through a knot in the wood on the front of the bar. Although she could not see his face, Katie knew it was Uncle Tommy. The black leather jacket with his club colors and rank, the black gloves with the Steelers logo and the smell of his Prince Matchabelli cologne were evidence. It was him. Once he landed, he did not move.

Just then, Katie heard the kitchen doors on the opposite side of the tap room swing and bang open, followed immediately by her mama's high pitched squealing scream. A bang of a gun, then more shouting about horses and money and a mustache. Mama cursed like Katie had never heard her do before. Words only men used and hateful to the core. It seemed she was not scared of these men at all, told them she didn't know anything about their horse's mustache or money Tommy owed them. She said that she kept out of the boys' business and they needed to get the fuck out of her tavern. Another pop of a gun and there was silence, all but the shuffling of the strangers' feet and knocking about the cash drawer near the kitchen doors.

Katie could not help herself. Sliding out of the hiding spot, crouching down behind the bar, she raised up, obscured by napkin holders and the like, to see the strangers. Two big, dark men with bushy beards and one smaller, squirrelly blonde guy with acne scars so plentiful she first thought he'd been burned. They wore leathers and club colors she didn't know. The squirrelly guy had the cash drawer out on the bar cursing over the lousy $100 it held. The big guys were in the tiny office next to the kitchen, rooting around and tossing things, bumping into each other. The slightly smaller, hairier of the two big guys turned out of the office doorway and barked orders at the other two to keep looking when Katie saw who he was. It was Moose, a friend of Aunt Gina's sometimes boyfriend Mike. Moose had been in the tavern many times since last summer. He had even come to the private invitation-only Christmas party and ate four plates of mama's secret recipe brisket. It was a special kind of insult to think that this asshole could eat her cooking for nearly a year, then have the nerve to do her like he did. It would have been easier coming from a stranger.

Suddenly, the panic hit her. Throughout the last few minutes or so, she knew enough to hide down low, but felt calm. She understood at once this was different, not a cash drawer dash, that Mama wasn't getting up. She began to freak out inside, wondering where Daddy and Aunt Gina were. By now, it was going on five in the afternoon. They were supposed to open the dining room and start serving dinner soon. They would have been there any other day. What happened to them? Where were they?

Katie swiveled round and bolted out the delivery door in the back, tore through the rear parking lot, jumped the cemetery fence, ran through the cemetery and a stand of woods until she was bursting through her own back door and into her mama's laundry room. It was wrecked! Everything was everywhere and the doors to the washer and dryer were hanging open. In the kitchen, the spicy smell from that morning's oatmeal clung to the air, and things were much the same disarray. Cupboard and cabinet doors hung open, dishes and food items were tossed about. The freezer and refrigerator doors hung open. Katie reached out and shut those out of habit. Even the oven and broiler doors were open.

"Daddy! Aunt Gina!" Katie yelled at the top of her lungs. She could hardly hear anything over the sound of her heart thumping in her chest. She had to walk farther into the house, into the living room, to hear another pounding *thump-thump-thump* coming from the sun porch out front. She followed the noise to find the dog bouncing his crate off of the floor, howling, trying to get out. Letting Freddy the hound dog out of his crate, she followed him into the garage. That is where she found her father, lying in a pool of blood, his face pale as elderberry blossom, barely breathing and nearly dead.

"Katie, I'm glad to see you!" Dutch O'Halloran managed to get out. "Run up into Chickaree mountain and hide. Don't come back for a couple days."

"But Daddy! What happened? Where's Aunt Gina and Mike?" Katie protested and began to slowly cry. "Uncle Tommy and Mama are in the tavern. They're shot. Papa! Who're those guys with Moose?"

"Girl, do what I tell you. There ain't no time for you to cry. This is soldier time! You have got to go now! Don't argue with me!" his voice stronger this time than last, a direct order. Katie knew what she had to do. "And Katie, take those bags of peanuts on my workbench with you." She watched his eyes look up and to his right. She rose, crossing over her daddy and took the crunchy brown paper bags into her hands.

"These, Daddy?" Katie turned to him, but he was gone. Freddy lay at his side, whining quietly. The good girl had no choice but to execute her Daddy's final orders. He said now and she would not disobey, no time for tears or other dramatics. Katie turned, hustled through the house, grabbing a gym bag into which she threw the peanut bags, a couple cans of Coke, a jar of crunchy peanut butter, a half loaf of bread and several books to occupy her for a few days. At the back door, she stopped, wondering if she should call the police or an ambulance. Daddy wouldn't have liked that idea. He hated the cops and the paramedics were only a slight step above. Besides, those paramedics weren't gonna be any good in this instance. Then, she heard the sirens. Mr. Gordon surely got out the side doors. She spotted Daddy's Woolrich jacket on the hook next to the door, grabbed it and started running again, Freddy following.

Sandi Keaton-Wilson

Poetic Injustice (Legal Degree)

Born to trouble
four generations
maybe more
of 'shine, shoot-outs,
synthetic drugs, meth...
He arrived with every
good gene from his
mama's side.
Pond blue eyes
looked beyond
the cloud shrouded mountains
far up into that dreaming place
one gets to by climbing
out of the ditch and over evil,
aiming for something other
than outlaw living.

Twelve years of school
with no absences,
no grade ever lower than the two B's
he got in Chemistry;
granted a full scholarship
for four years at the best university.
Borrowing his uncle's red Camaro;
Roy , the youngest of his papaw's boys,
wouldn't be needing it
pulling ten in the state pen.

Predestined to be pulled over
by bird-dogging law enforcement,
their canine unit
sniffing out unknown, long-hidden cocaine.
He was arrested, no one attested that
the boy was clean. Now he's
doing plenty enough time before he's free
to earn a four year degree.

Richard Childers

Like Fire on Your Throat

The clearing is thick with weeds and brush. You can tell it's been a blue moon since we've visited our hideaway in the woods.

James is my older cousin by two years. In eight months he'll be able to get his driver license. He has green eyes, but the white around his pupils has a dirty yellow tinge to it that reminds me of walls in a chain smoker's house. His greasy black hair curls up when summer comes around and the air gets sticky. He likes to brag that his hair is truly black because his daddy has Indian blood in him.

"You know its gonna burn, right? You can't be a pussy." James swings his legs off the four-wheeler and is at the toolbox in two cocky bounces. It's one of those toolboxes that sit in the back of a pickup truck. Not a nice metal one, but a big clunky plastic one as black as James' Indian hair. He throws the lid open and reaches in.

At first I think his stepdad just has some damn good stuff. He sits on the ground a few feet away from the toolbox, a flash of gold slithers away into the weeds. I reckon the copperhead hit him a pretty good lick. He's holding his neck tight and breathing like he caught a peek up a girl's skirt. He's trying to say something to me, but can't get the words out. Whatever he had for dinner is all over my Nikes. I step back a few feet. That's about all I can manage. After he pukes for a spell he lies down and starts holding his sides, sore from all the gagging.

He's lying there on his back kicking dirt and grabbing at patches of weeds around him. Like a spider that's been half stepped on, but still has some life in it. His eyes look about ready to pop out of his head begging for help, but the way the sun is hitting those dark green pupils he looks like he's right where he belongs.

The white pocket tee he's wearing has dirt and grass

stains all up the back from him thrashing around on the forest floor like a wild hog. His bangs are plastered to his forehead with sweat and the place where he's bitten is swelled up and bruising.

I can hear a bird somewhere up above chirping; pleading with me to wake up. The four-wheeler idles behind me like a storm coming up over the mountain. What light makes its way down through the screen of leaves and branches above hits the ground with a dull thud. Over the hill James' dad is knocking the bottom out of a Budweiser. His mom is sitting at their computer cross-eyed, "liking" pictures of Jesus on her Facebook.

For a second I think about lying down next to my cousin and seeing the world from his point of view. I bet those poplar trees look like they shoot straight into Heaven.

Wendy Dinwiddie

The Box and the Machine

The first time I met my Uncle Mull, Momma and Daddy brought him home from the dentist. The blood dried down from the corners of his mouth in broad lines. The skin of his cheek was puffed and mottled. The whole right side of his face swoll up like he'd been saving all of our conversations there, like he'd brought in the drag of his jaw some secret from the other side of the world.

He'd hung his head out the cracked window of Momma's El Dorado. The thin angle of his arm jutted out into the afternoon. Steel hair pulled back from his face in wild wisps. He rattled up the drive with the sun hot against his Percocet bottle.

Momma slung the car up to the front steps, and Daddy was out of the back before she'd put it in park. She leaned out across Uncle Mull, eyes on the house.

"He's your brother," she said.

Daddy never smiled, but this was a whole new kind of not smiling. His mouth set rough against its own edges.

"He's not staying," Daddy said. He didn't look back as he took the steps.

Uncle Mull embroidered cats on all our sweaters with a machine he'd found listed on the back page of the Thrifty Nickel. He sat in the cool dark cave of our living room with the machine's guts autopsied across the coffee table, smoked Pall Malls and stitched tabbies. He ran the thing on into the night, kept us all awake with its screams. The needle jumped the track about every twentieth stitch, and he'd cuss and creak up from the La-Z-Boy and rethread it. Sometimes his yellow hands shook so bad that he'd stumble to my room and shove me awake. The moon bare on the brown carpet. His eyes red-laced in the dark. The whole house quiet.

He brought me to the machine most nights that summer, let me watch their little whiskers come to life, the soft bend of their paws, the pink pads of their feet, the crook of each ear placed over the sweater's left breast like they lived through our heartbeats. Their eyes were old and new, sometimes a rich purple and sometimes a bright gold that the lady in the catalog called Autumn Sun.

I never heard the cats speak, but I knew that when I wasn't with them, when it was just him and the machine, they moved. They danced and spoke and told such lonely secrets from the mouths of things just made that I crept through the quiet house with my ears always open.

Uncle Mull stitched one of Momma's sweaters up with a special pack he'd ordered from the catalog's insert. Fall in New England. He threaded a narrow running stitch into the crook of a hundred tiny leaves, a whole forest of trees decked in thick flame-colored taffeta party dresses and among their roots a litter of lithe young kittens played, their paws cross-stitched full of flutes and harps and a long flat stringed instrument that Momma said was a dulcimer. He left it sitting out on the kitchen table when the sun hadn't yet risen above the distant caps of the ridge.

Momma traced her fingers over the embroidery. She took it into the laundry room off the back of the house and slid the sweater down over her head. Slow and gentle, like it wasn't that same sweater that had lived with her all the cold long winters that I could remember.

One afternoon, Momma and I found Uncle Mull with his head slumped over the arm of the La-Z-Boy, his mouth hung open. His cigarette burned a hole in the recliner. A one-eyed kitten waved at us from the edge of a copse of trees, the other eye a faint outline, the same milky yellow as the fabric underneath.

Momma moved without speaking, arranged Uncle Mull in his chair until I would have thought he'd fallen asleep there in that space between morning and afternoon. Her hands were careful. She didn't look over at me.

"Don't tell your father," she said.

I didn't.

Momma said that Uncle Mull used the pills to keep whatever it was that Daddy hated inside. He told it to the machine. Momma refused to buy us any more sweaters, so when Uncle Mull finished with the last of them, he started in on the curtains.

I broke down boot boxes and taped them flat to the corners of my window. They kept the morning sun from coming in. Every other window in the house stood bare and blue. Momma scrubbed the panes until the glass glittered. She sang Patty Loveless and Loretta Lynn while she worked. It was the happiest I'd ever seen her.

Some days, the other kids at school wanted to watch Uncle Mull drink his way through Daddy's after supper Budweiser. He'd bring his beer onto the porch and lift up the right corner of his shirt to show us all a long-seamed scar he said he got in a knife fight on Mud Island, but Daddy said was from having his appendix taken out. He had other scars, too, most of them as thin and white as spider webs, sewn up his arms and down his legs and a few stitched at the crook of his left elbow.

When Daddy came home to find half of my seventh grade class on the gray porch listening to a story about Blues musicians and river barges, he got mad, pushed us all back into the dust of the road, and then at the turn by the maple and the mailbox, we heard him screaming.

The first time I saw Daddy put his fist through the wall, Uncle Mull had slid off the couch. A dark wet stain spread onto the carpet around him. The room smelled sour.

Daddy stood in the doorway, his shoulders held tight under the cover of his work shirt. He curled the dark crescents of his nails into his palms, balled up his knuckles into the ridges of a fist. The muscles on the insides of his wrists bulged out.

Budweiser cans lined the coffee table two rows deep. One of Momma's salad plates perched atop it, full of ashes. Daddy stood there until the living room grew small around us, and I itched. I pulled at the sleeves of my jacket. There was something of the devil in Uncle Mull, and it was trying its best to get out.

Daddy moved into the room. His steps shook the glass in the china cabinet. He grabbed Uncle Mull under his arms and hefted him onto the couch, head lolled down onto his shoulder.

Daddy pinned him there with his good hand and turned to look at me.

"Where's your mother?" he said.

I ran back into the belly of the house.

Uncle Mull stopped waking me up in the middle of the night to untangle the machine. I would lie awake far into the dark listening to the whirring gobble of the needle, to the creak of the La-Z-Boy's springs, to the slam of the screen door when he went out onto the dark porch. He took to driving the El Dorado over back roads at night. I'd go to the window of my room and push back the cardboard to watch the one good headlight trace across the silver grass.

One night, he ran the car back over our long driveway, the lone spotlight like the eye of some monster tracking up the road.

The screen door popped soft against the frame, and in the shadow of yellow from the kitchen, Momma walked, wrapped up in Uncle Mull's sweater. Her legs were tall marble columns in the moonlight. Her feet bare. Her hair draped in a thick braid over her right shoulder.

Uncle Mull cut the engine, and for a while the only sound was the ticking of the metal as it cooled. Then he got out of the car and leaned up against the driver's door. He lit another cigarette. Momma treaded the watery distance between them. She unhooked her arms and laid her body along Uncle Mull's, and when they kissed slow, I dropped back from the window and stood behind its veil, listening to my own lonely breathing.

Daddy took all of our sweaters and put them in a big moving box in the corner of the living room. He guarded that box. He marked its place up against the baseboards with a piece of masking tape. He kept on adding. He hunted through closets and drawers and those old battered suitcases where Momma kept our snow clothes. The sweaters and curtains and all the rest spilled over the top and onto the floor, and still Uncle Mull ran the machine, and still Daddy searched.

I came home from school one day, and Momma's El Dorado wasn't slung up against the side of the house, and all the doors and windows were shut up. I walked through the empty rooms. Momma had left the iron skillet full of gravy and water in the sink. She'd left clothes in the washing machine.

I grabbed a sweater out of the box, a black and orange calico, and went onto the porch to wait. By the time Daddy got home, the sunset had settled its wide blanket over the valley, the tops of the trees haloed in pink. Daddy pulled the truck up to the front steps. He put it in park and left the lights trained on me. He didn't make to get out.

I saw him open his Red Man pouch and slide another plug of tobacco behind his cheek. Then he just looked at me long and hard.

He sat there looking at me until the sun had gone

down, and the cab of the truck was dark, and I couldn't see him staring. Then I heard the engine crank and the gears shift, and he swung the truck in a big wide arch and kicked up gravel on his way back into town.

It finally got too cold to sit out there, so I went in and sat on the couch with my knees jutted up against the coffee table with the box and the machine.

When Daddy still went to church with us, Momma wore her hair all piled up on the top of her head. The thin white cords of her neck curled into the curve of her shoulder. She wore dresses the color of hearthfire and gardenia perfume, and while the preacher spoke from Solomon and Psalms, Daddy'd rest his hand on the back of her head, trace the line of her hair with the broadside of his thumb or the curl of his knuckle. He'd sing "At the Cross" in pants with perfect creases, and we'd all go out for fried chicken with Momma's Sunday School class.

Daddy says he doesn't believe in God anymore.

Before dawn worked its way through the gaps in the shoeboxes, I woke to Daddy's rough hand on my arm.

"Irene," he said. "Irene, get up." His shoulders cut the space like tired furniture. "We're going to town."

I slid out of the bed. Everything wore the young haze of sleep. In the light of the moon, he cast shadows on the wall.

Daddy hefted both arms under the box. The cold air nipped its way up my shirt sleeves, the gray light of morning a pale puddle over the scrub grass and jimson weed and gnarled veins of the yard. I hugged my elbows closer.

Daddy put the box in the bed of the Dodge, spit out the tobacco juice he'd been holding.

"Get in the truck," he said. He wiped his hands down the front of his jacket, left a trail of dust on both sides of the zipper.

We made it to the turn by the mailbox before the light crept into the cab. The sun played across Daddy's hands white-knuckled on the steering wheel. The cab smelled thick and sweet like antifreeze. I waited. We sat there with the signal blinking and the heat blasting. My eyes watered. I cracked the window. Daddy turned left toward town.

The night that Daddy found Uncle Mull on the floor, the screen door popped and pulled, and I got out of bed and went onto the front porch. Uncle Mull sat on the steps staring out at the yard. The silver web of trees glittered under the November moon, their branches naked against the cold. Uncle Mull lit the first of a train of Pall Malls and handed it to me through the rails.

The smoke burned its way down into my lungs and then back up. I started coughing.

He'd found one of Daddy's sweatshirts with the logo for the tire factory stitched over the right breast. A yellow tomcat kneaded his claws onto the small of the sweater's back. The whites of its eyes shone. My voice was lost somewhere out there in the dark.

"Why?" I said after a while.

"Irene," he said. "Don't make the mistake of thinking your Daddy knows everything." He tugged his knees up close to him on the steps. "He don't."

When he turned to me, I saw the skin around his right eye was puffed and purple in the curl of cigarette smoke. He'd pulled his hair back, still damp from the shower.

I knew, in a way I'd never known with Daddy, that he was telling me the truth.

Outside the truck, the trees drew sentinel along the road. We drove in their long latticed shadows. The river ran steady to our left. The whole world outside the cab quiet. In the bed, the box knocked over and slid up against the side.

"He ain't right in the head," Daddy said. "He's never been right."

I saw the cuts on Daddy's knuckles. Last night's anger still on his breath. Not for the first time, the man my father was scared me.

Daddy and I rode on into the silence. The truck's bearings squeaking out over every dip and bump in the road. The cover of ice melted from the side window like a tideline receding. I tried to decide if he wanted me to speak, wanted me to say Momma wasn't going to be there when we got back.

"I would've loved her," he said. "I would've kept on loving her until I died if it hadn't been for that man back there."

I was headed toward crying, so I didn't say anything. It felt like my mouth was stem-stitched shut, the floss pulled tight through the hooks of my lips.

"I don't blame your Momma," Daddy said. "I lived for a long time thinking he was a different man."

Last night, he and Momma must have got all of their screaming out on the ride back. They spoke in closed-off voices. They spoke in whispers. They spoke from the other side of a great long time, the years of their relationship drawn so thin that the conversation could only scrape through between them.

Momma was still wearing that same sweater. The skirt of a blood orange dress peeking out underneath. She had her shoes in her hand, and there was a run in the calf of her hose.

Daddy had her big quilted overnight bag strapped over his right shoulder. Her eyes caught mine. They were red.

"Go to bed, Irene," Momma said.

Under my pillow was a half-empty pack of Pall Malls.

We pulled into the dump, and there was a big chain on the gate. Daddy left the truck running and picked his way over the yard. He climbed the front steps and knocked on the door of the trailer. An old man came out in a green housecoat. He watched us.

Daddy unlocked the gate and got back in the truck. He pulled up alongside the dumpster.

The box waited in the back, full to its brim with tabbies and torties, calicos and Siamese. Their eyes round and golden. I knew they watched the shadowy seams for any change in the pattern of light. I knew they were afraid.

Daddy got out and bent his body down over the bed. He picked up the box. I squeezed my eyes shut.

After awhile, I heard the creak of the door, felt the dip of Daddy's weight on the bench. The whole world tilted toward him and then righted itself. Everything stretched out pale in that space between us.

"It would have been different if it was the first time," he said, more to the steering wheel and the trees than to me. "But it wasn't."

Over by an old refrigerator, a dog sniffed at the gravel, turned, squatted on its spotted haunches. I wondered if it belonged to the old man in the trailer. I had put away some quiet part of myself in the stillness. I pressed my cheek to the icy window, tried to call it back. Daddy started the truck and took us home.

Daniel Stephenson

Hank Don't

Hank don't
float without
3 beers in him and meth
makes you sink like a hole dumbfuck
of our spit up in long sentences: Life. Boats
in flotsam/
jetsam fishing for tired arms tied in like universe
mobiles, turned up
tires and wormed out
trash.

"Rape, possession" Hank says and I'm
                    lost: You're dusted
                                    by a cup of crystal
                                    tongues, a salt
                                        lake of taste
                                            buds dried
                                            to your leg hair like white
                                        aphids. Your imprints
thighed with tomato suckers. I don't remember
etching nerve into glass
glances up
stream. Another
hooker, another boat. A sentence lit
in surface wires of Bud Lights
bobbing loose, bobbing

loose. Hank's snagged
an old hood and broke
in memory
of the price of scrap gone up and why
we're here fishing for shit in goose crap in our baseball caps for
money on a Sunday; why
clouds don't freebase this
muddy stream and sneeze sepia,
blowing our ears out into empty light
beer cans crimped in with all the odds
and ends I know?
I don't know.

Michael Henson

All This Craziness

(A story from *The Way the World Is: the Maggie Boylan Stories*, first published by Brighthorse Books)

Corey Hacker leaned out over her porch rail and peered once more up the road and into the dark.

"She'll come home when she wants to come home," her husband said from the door. "Come on in before you catch your death of cold."

"Hush," she said. "Wait a minute." Her voice was sharp. Sharper than she intended, but there it was. She was lean as an axe handle and her eye was sharp as her words. She cut him a look with the blade of her eye, hoping he would back off.

"Let her go," he said. "She's grown."

"She's not grown."

"She's twenty-two years old. She's grown. She can do what she wants. I did what I wanted when I was twenty-two. And so did you."

And look where it got us, she wanted to say. Donald was a preacher now, but he had been in a biker gang when he was younger and he had the scars and the tattoos and the crooked-leg limp to prove it. She had left her first husband for this man and his tattoos—the scars and the crushed leg came later. She remembered that and took her sharp eye away.

"She's still a baby to me," she said.

"She had her own mind when she was a baby," he said. "Even before all this craziness."

Craziness: Sheila, her daughter, her only, her hope and her heart, the child of her own crazy youth, The girl had taken to running the roads late of a night, making all the wrong decisions with all the wrong people, running afoul of the law and good sense. She had dropped the college scholarship and picked up the wild boyfriend, the wild moods, the tattoos and the piercings, and the OxyContin, the crazy cause of it all.

"I thought she quit for good this time," her mother said. "I really thought for sure she would quit."

"You don't need to wait out here anyway," Donald said. "You'll hear that muffler long before you see any headlights."

"In and out of treatment, how many times? In and out of jail? You'd think she would have learned from all we went through. And now this business of testifying against her so-called best friend. You'd think," she said. "You'd think she'd start to see it."

He said nothing to that. He held the door open and waited.

She noticed the silence and thought, he knows something and he's not about to say it. It set her to pondering in the back yard of her mind.

She peered over the porch rail one more time, then followed him into the house. He was right; it was the dead of night, it was the dead of winter. It was too late, too cold to be watching for a set of headlights that might not come at all.

He told her goodnight and limped off to bed. "I'll be up directly, she told him. She had to be at work first thing; she needed to get some sleep. But first, she settled into a kitchen chair. She loosened her hair from its clips and bands. She took a brush from the pocket of her gown and began to brush her hair. It fell nearly to the floor and she brushed it out and brushed it out and then put the hairbrush down, pulled her hair back, divided it into three strands, then wove the strands into a long, thick braid.

He knows something, she thought. He's been talking to that courthouse crowd and he knows something but he won't say what he knows.

And she would have asked, but by the time she came to bed, her husband had fallen asleep with his Bible collapsed in front of him and his big hands splayed out like fallen pillars.

She slept, but she did not sleep long. Some time before

dawn, she heard the ragged rumble of the muffler coming down the road and up the drive, then a shuffle and a stumble and a whisper of voices and she got up to check.

Sheila and her wild boyfriend stood in her bedroom in front of her dresser, stuffing clothes and cosmetics into a duffel. A backpack and a spangled purse, already filled, waited by the door. They were working in the light of a small study lamp. So when Corey turned on the overhead light, they both stood startled, half blind, and blinking.

"What the f—!" The boyfriend saw who it was and broke off.

Her daughter did not. "Ma! What the fuck? Are you trying to blind us?

"What's going on?"

"Can you tell?"

"It looks like you're packing to leave."

"That's exactly what I'm doing."

"Your dad'll not be happy."

"Donald's not my dad."

"He'll do till you find you a better one."

"I got to go, Ma. Maggie Boylan's gonna kick my ass if she sees me."

"She's gonna see you at five in the morning?"

"Not yet, but she will."

"Because you testified against her?"

"She's trying to say I lied on her."

"Did you?"

"Did I what?"

"Did you tell a lie on Maggie Boylan?"

"Did Donald tell you I did?"

"He never said a word. I just want to know. Did you lie on Maggie Boylan?"

"Ma, I can't believe you're even asking me such a thing."

"Did you?" The notion had festered and now she needed to know.

"I'm not going through this all over again."

"All I did was ask. And you can't give me a straight answer. That says a lot."

"It says I'm tired of you and your nosy questions."

"As long as you're living under my roof, I got a right to an answer."

"Ma, I got to go. Maggie's looking for me. And when I'm gone, you can keep your roof for yourself"

"Donald's here. He's not gonna let you come to any harm."

"Donald's gonna say, let her suffer the natural consequences."

"Maggie Boylan's not a natural consequence."

"No, she's a natural disaster and I got to get out of the way."

Corey nodded toward the boyfriend. "You got all the disaster you need right there. He's a one-man catastrophe."

"Ma, don't start." She emptied the last drawer into the duffel and hitched it to her shoulder.

"Let me see your eyes," Corey said. "I want to see does he have you on something."

"Ma, I'm not your little girl anymore."

"Let me see your eyes."

"Ma, no."

The mother squinted up her own eyes to see better. She even turned the beam of the study lamp on her daughter's face. "Let me see," she said. Her word and eye were sharp again.

"Come on, Ronnie, we got to get out of here," the daughter said.

The woman stepped to block her daughter's path.

"Ma! Have you gone totally crazy?"

The boyfriend looked from mother to daughter with eyes big as dollar coins.

"Corey, let her go." Donald was limping down the hall.

"Ma, I swear. If you don't get out of the way, I'm gonna knock you right down the stairs."

"I want to see your eyes."

"Let her go," Donald said. "Just let her pass."

"Do what he says, Ma. For once in your life, do the sensible thing."

Her husband took her by the shoulder and started to guide her backwards out of their path.

She didn't fight him; she knew she had lost this battle long ago.

"Go on," Corey said. "There's nothing ever gonna be right in this world. You might as well be wrong with the rest."

"This is crazy," said the daughter. "This whole family is crazy."

"If you leave," the mother said, "you ain't comin back."

"If I leave, you're right. I'm not ever coming back. I don't want to ever come back to this crazy house."

Corey started to flare back; the words were right at the gate of her teeth. But she knew there was nothing more to say. She let her husband pull her back further down the hall. Sheila and Ronnie lifted the duffle and the backpack and trundled them down the stairs.

Corey turned away. She shrugged her husband's hands off her shoulders and stared away where she could not see them leave.

They stood in the hall for several long minutes as the girl and her boyfriend stumbled their plunder down the steps. They heard the trundlethump at each step, then the creak of the porch boards, and the throaty roar of Sheila's perforated muffler as they scratched and rumbled out the drive and down the road.

"I thought you was gonna fix that muffler," the mother said.

"There's a lot of things I ain't yet fixed," he said. They stood in the dark hall and talked mufflers and rain gutters and all manner of things in need of fixing.

They spoke in a hush, at a bare whisper, though there really was no need.

Christopher McCurry

It Begins

No revolution without blood.

So, too, the newborn
caked in the
red of her mother.

The cat's split lip proceeds the death of the rabbit
and the cocooned sleep thereafter.

Why is it that
all that is soft
is sheared
for further use?

All these men in their thick coats carry disaster in them.

Their ears
turned to hunks
of shrapnel
above the collar.

Here's what they say to one another in the street,
their eyes skittish:

When the world is too much
drop the deathball--
it will be a labor too.

Charles A. Swanson

A Journey for Flowers

We were in woods of winter's bleakened trees—
Going to dig old flower bulbs—she and I.
I pushed a blue wheelbarrow. She stepped high,
Her britches scraping on her skinny knees.
The day was rare—white sun had thawed the freeze
And sifted down like resting fireflies.
Winter brought us hunger for blue skies,
For spring sunshine and cedar-scented breeze—
Down the disused road on stretches of old brick,
Through a mile of woods behind the Chesick place,
The land owned now by Continental Can,
To the old house site where daffodils grew thick,
And coy blue stars of periwinkle traced
A fading imprint of the hand of man.

Ashleigh Gill

On the Kanawha River Oil and Chemical Spills, Charleston, WV

The river burned, Kanawha sleek and old,
the bather and the drinker burned.
The river was a gray-lunged mule, and then
it was a soup bone, and then
it was the sweet-breathed shudder in the pipes
that kept the children up, saying,
"If I cannot be water
then I will be war."
Farther south, it slipped
its patient hands along
the hulls of boats and through the hair
of water-wary girls.
When it was hungry, it took,
with the slow, fossil
vengeance of water.

Clyde Kessler

Nearing Winter Solstice

December scratches the old dam
where it failed. Mud and slush
are pushing downstream like torn quilts
while sleet rattles against a drain pipe.

My sister jumps between willows.
Our mutt rousts up a meadowlark.
And in what's left of the pond, a grebe
disappears in the water. It's magic,
daddy calls it mud duck trickery.

And here along Eaker Branch, the fog
is gnawing away the woods and fields,
all of it forcing winter into our nerves,
except we're kids, and we laugh,
and jump the creek again.

Aaron Morris

Kanawha County, West Virginia, 2014

They're saying that it smells like licorice,
The chemical that seeped into the stream,
Preventing us from bathing or washing our hands.
Like saccharine whiskey, fumes perfume the road,
Itself a grizzled string of licorice,
Its granite grooves each marked by slow sedans
That scoot ahead in search of fresh water.
Suddenly, so many things resemble sweets.
Throughout the water bottles' emptied shelves
In the Dollar Tree, the tiny holes that fill
Their metallic backs are licorice gumdrops.
The setting sun is blinding butterscotch
That, scattered on the windshield, makes it hard
To drive. Even the coal the chemical
Had washed is just a rinsed-off chocolate
That fell on the floor. Austere beside the river,
The storage tubs of Freedom Industries
Don't need the colors of our jelly beans
To hide behind, merely a nom de plume
Of liberation.

Eventually, I go
To a gas stop's convenience store. Before,
When I had visited the Dollar Tree,
I overheard reports of fighting
At other stores: pushing, then fists, a fall
To frenzy for some jugs of water.
Now, entering the gas stop, I see
A man place bottles on the counter and turn
Around for more. I nearly run to the back,
And I think I've lost when he beats me there,
Opens the cooler door, and offers me

Two bottles, saying I can take some more
If I need them. His hazel eyes reveal
A sweetness that transcends our candy's smell.

Rebecca S. Lindsay

Black's Run

They've built an interstate through my childhood,
paved over the halcyon days with tar,
constructed an overpass where bellowing semis
fracture the hush, the din of rolling rubber
obscures the suck and gurgle of rush over rock.

Still, as you fly over, you can lower
the glass and filter the wind, strain from it
these ever echoes:
    the swish of the swing,
    the ricochet of olly-olly-oxen-free,
    the splatter of the flat stone skipping,
    the chatter of dreams.

Rhonda Pettit

Finding Buried Creek

"There will have to be concern...with the watersheds of unspectacular streams..."
—*Wendell Berry,* Unforeseen Wilderness

One Saturday on our way to a Community of Writers workshop taking place along the Ohio River, my older brother Jay and I were driving on Route 2398 in Campbell County, Kentucky, through an area nicknamed Little Appalachia. This narrow, two-lane road winds its way up a ridge from the Licking River valley, and feels much farther away than the few miles that separate it from Highland Heights, Newport, and Cincinnati. A small creek runs beside and sometimes under it. The houses here are fewer and older, nesting among the slopes, and many have substantial gardens, barns, and critters. While we were absorbing the rural charm of this area, Jay claimed that people who live along a river have a life and identity different from anything he and I know, having grown up in a Kentucky suburb of Cincinnati. He didn't say *independent*, but that was the word that came to mind as river life and mountain life began to merge.

Being in constant contact with a force of nature, like a river, would certainly lend independence to a person. What is more independent than a river – it both makes and *is* its own passage, direction, obstacles, and escapes. In our journey that day we were traveling through a landscape that two rivers and their web of creeks, among other forces, had helped and continue to shape. We crossed the ridge top at Route 27, descended the other side toward the Ohio River valley, and headed south on Route 8 along the river toward our workshop. Later that day, one of the writing prompts we were given by poet Richard Hague was: Write Your River Autobiography. I didn't think I had one.

Born in Northern Kentucky, I have lived within ten miles of the Ohio and Licking rivers for most of my life, have crossed those rivers many times, but never in my childhood or early adulthood did I feel a close affinity to them. They were known to be polluted: don't drink the water, don't eat the fish, don't swim. What was the point, then, of fishing or camping there, or having a boat on those filthy waters? The lexicon of high school athletics didn't help. Rival teams from schools that were located along the Ohio or Licking were called "river rats." If we couldn't defeat them on the field, we would beat them up with vocabulary. On top of which, my parents weren't drawn to the river the way some of the other families we knew were, in part because of the expense in time and money a boat required. And every summer, children and adults drowned in one of the five rivers in the greater Cincinnati area. My parents also had witnessed, individually from the safety of a Devou Park hillside, the 1937 flood, and likely remembered the smoke if not the flames of burning gasoline on Mill Creek. Large destructive floods like those of 1913, 1927, and 1937 can saturate the public memory with fear. I suspect that for my parents, the word *river* raised red flags and worry, as well as the kind of respect that kept them at a distance from potentially raging waters.
It seems strange to have been so disconnected from the rivers when we were a family that loved water in our own way. Like many Baby Boom families, we went to Florida every summer in the 1950s and 60s to be near the ocean. Jay and I swam often in our neighborhood's private pool. For a few years in his twenties, he would have a boat and share a cabin on the Ohio with his friends, but I was too young at the time to be included in those adventures, and I remained indifferent about rivers; they were something to cross, not enter.

This attitude changed somewhat when I was a student at the University of Kentucky in the mid-1970s. The state and U. S. Army Corps of Engineers were threatening to dam the

Red River in eastern Kentucky to create a recreational lake out of the Red River Gorge. I read Wendell Berry's *The Unforeseen Wilderness* – an extended essay about the gorge, and one of the first books I bought that wasn't required for a course – and hiked and camped in the Red River Gorge with friends. But there was no transcendence from that rich experience, which would continue over the twelve years I lived in Lexington after graduation, to the rivers of home.

From the age of five I grew up on a creek – a small one – that went the way of many creeks in Northern Kentucky subject to post-World War II development. The low hills it flowed through in the small cities of Erlanger and Elsmere became a series of houses and subdivisions, and the creek, bearing no name that I had ever heard, became a line in their storm sewer system, partially buried beneath our street and some of the yards. Once I was old enough to appreciate how these systems functioned, using the word *creek* for our little exposure of water sounded inaccurate and sentimental. Could an urban stream used as a storm sewer line be more than just a conveyor of pollutants? Yet where it surfaced in our yard and in the yard across the street and two doors up, the creek in the early 1960s was both adventure and laboratory to kids in the neighborhood. Its banks and waters offered a habitat of frogs and tadpoles, turtles, black snakes, garter snakes, snails, minnows, and crawdads. The three-foot concrete pipe into which it disappeared in our yard and re-emerged in the other was, for me at least, a dark cave where the Furies resided.

In spite of the creek, and the woods and hills that ringed our neighborhood, I identified myself as a girl from the city, albeit a small city, and the North. My education came from a city school. My news and entertainment media came from Cincinnati, the City of Seven Hills with a growing urban Appalachian population. Perhaps because those hills were associated with ancient Rome rather than the far more ancient Appalachian mountains, several Queen City radio personalities thought it appropriate to joke about “Kentucky hillbillies.” I felt the insult but denied the label. Like rivers, hills for me were simply an obstruction – something to get over or around – not an identity.

Recently I traced the creek upstream through what remains of the old woods behind my childhood home. I realized that it extends under the low point of Dell Street, a narrow, residential street that runs from the top of one steep hill at the edge of Erlanger to the top of another one in Elsmere. Beyond the bottom of Dell Street, the creek must have flowed through a long-gone farm in the small valley between hills, on the other side of the street. The farm had been a little piece of country entirely surrounded by individual homes and ongoing development in Elsmere. The number of rural holdouts within city limits was diminishing in the 1960s, but a few non-farmer residents kept vegetable gardens as well as rabbits and chickens. The sound of a cock crowing in the morning punctuated my first few years at our house, but it wasn’t coming from the Dell Street farm. Roosters were elsewhere.

As a pre-adolescent I used to walk to the farm with my friend Melissa to buy vegetables in the summer. I can still smell the damp dark earth beneath the three-walled shed where tomatoes, green peppers, cucumbers, beans, and corn were laid across an old plank table. They were warm from having been that day in the sun, and the greenness of their ripe scents mingled with that of the dirt floor. These scents and colors and textures might explain why, years later, I would relate immediately to Theodore Roethke’s poem, “Root Cellar,” where “Even the dirt kept breathing a small breath.” We didn’t have a root cellar at my house; we had a “finished basement,” meaning: a downstairs living space.

I don’t remember seeing the creek on the farm property as we walked the dirt driveway to the shed, but I remember the woman who lived there and sold us the produce. She was heavy-set with small dark eyes, high cheekbones, and yellowish-gray hair pulled slick and tight into a bun. A thin cotton dress always hugged the top and bottom rounds of her body. She was very tan, said little, never smiled. Her body carried the scent of sun-work, garden-sweat more earthy than pungent. Though I had been taught it was rude to stare, I couldn't take my eyes off of her, even when I wasn't looking directly at her. I wonder how she might have interpreted my rudeness. If I hadn't stared at her, though, she might not be with me now. I never knew her name or anything about her life, but remembering her feels necessary, is perhaps a kind of reverence. After all, my family ate her food during the late summer months; we were connected to her by those vegetables and the creek our properties shared across city limits.

Back then I was blind to my home geography. I knew about Dell Street (and *the farmer in the dell*) but not *dell* as in *a small secluded valley or glen, usually a wooded one*. I defaulted to imagination instead of the dictionary. In my nine-year-old mind the creek disappeared beyond my house into deep woods that I was not supposed to enter alone. I wasn't aware that our street, a cul-de-sac ending with a members-only swimming pool, transected the valley through which the creek ran, though I had run through this valley, stared at it from the house and yard, played in it with kids from a street full of large Catholic families, and found some of my first fossils in it.

After I became obsessed with fossil collecting in my early teens, my geography was the Ordovician Sea, and the creek became a lesser body of water to the one I imagined in the shale and limestone. Though fossilized, there was more animal life represented in the rock than I was finding alive in the creek by then. The real Furies were the pollutants in the water. Today the creek tends to offer home to discarded items from the careless neighbors upstream, where a new apartment complex was planted on the hill above the creek before it disappears under Dell Street. A senior center and more apartments sit where the farm was, all of this happening while I lived and worked elsewhere. After years and towns away, I had come back with my husband Mike to live in the house and creek I grew up in, having landed a tenure-track position at the University of Cincinnati. I began to take better notice of the property and our "unspectacular stream," its former and current conditions. In the process, I gave our nameless creek a name: Buried Creek.

"I think this house wants you to write about it," Mike told me, not long after we moved into the house on Buried Creek. I had begun a series of narrative poems about a World War II veteran, using my father, who died when I was sixteen, as a model. My poems would take this character from his childhood on a farm, through college and his war experience, to his post-war life in the 1960s. My research for this project has taken me to university libraries, county deed offices, my father's college textbooks from the 1930s, my paternal grandmother's scrapbooks, genealogy records, and the steeply ridged farmland of Pendleton County, Kentucky. This work continues, and one of its many gifts was learning that the farm my father grew up on, sold when his father died in 1942, bordered the Licking River, not far from where its two forks join in Falmouth.

When I was a child, one of my father's Sunday refrains was, "Let's take a drive to Falmouth!" The four of us would pile into our 1957 gray Pontiac, sometimes with my maternal grandparents, and head south to see both the farm and the county seat. Falmouth was beginning to suffer from the isolation caused by the end of train travel – the L&N No. 38 local run to Cincinnati didn't stop there anymore – and the construction of Interstate-75 about fifteen miles to the west. But as a word, *Falmouth* symbolized my father's past and the farm. I don't recall the details of those trips. If he ever mentioned the river in connection with the farm, the image coursed its way beyond my attention. I know he didn't mention the fact, if he knew it, that his great-grandparents, Absalom (a farmer, tanner, and Justice of the Peace in 1858) and Elizabeth Hart Pettit, were baptized in the Licking. This image was another resonating gift from research. All I knew was that when he was sixteen my father couldn't wait to leave the farm, and he did, becoming an insurance agent, realtor, and police court judge after college and the war. Absalom's triplicate of occupations echoed in my father's life. Looking back, though, I also see how his farm time along the Licking and its creeks had rivered itself into his being.

My parents had their reasons for buying this house – escape from a noisy neighborhood and the maintenance of an older house, the private swim club associated with the new house – but learning about my father's link to the Licking River added another one. The house, a small 1959 ranch, was built into a hill on nearly an acre of hilly, wooded land that bottomed out at the creek. This property must have struck a chord, whether my father was conscious of it or not, with the farm where he was raised. In his healthy years he would ring the house with flowers, especially roses, and plant tomatoes every summer. His patch of orange daylilies bloomed along the creek. As older trees died he planted new ones, including an Arbor Day redbud sapling I brought home from school when I was seven or eight; we planted it together in the backyard, uphill from the creek along our property line. He sawed and stacked wood for winter fires in the fireplace. He cut the grass on his riding mower like a farmer plowing his fields, also using the mower to smooth the ground by pulling a metal roller once or twice a year. After hard spring and summer rains, he would sweep standing water out of our basement without complaint. When a developer and the city wanted to extend the street through our backyard to a subdivision that would soon take the woods behind our house and our side of the street, my father fought them off – I'm not sure how. He was protecting the land that was our home, though he couldn't save the woods. Some part of him was still farming along the river.

As I read more about the Licking, I learned that my father's connection to a river with severe meanderings in Pendleton County is a meandering connection to Appalachia. The Licking River's headwaters in Magoffin County mean that it springs from an area that had been heavily logged before it was heavily mined, and thus subject to the damages caused by both. No doubt cleaner when my father lived near it than it is now, the Licking brings with its pollutants the grit and gravel from its mountain source, and beyond that, a rich history before and after the Ice Age. Humans and other animals sought its salt licks, its fish, its water, and its passage. Through my father, I was part of that river, its headwaters and its mountain. My Pettit ancestors were among the pioneer families who pushed through the Appalachians from Virginia in the 1700s, and there are Pettits who remained in the mountains, though I haven't yet discovered a relative there. Of course, I am connected to the Appalachian Mountains regardless of my father's origins, given the essential role they play in eastern U. S. ecology, but my new river knowledge led me to a relationship that is both personal and universal. As bell hooks put it in her introduction to *Appalachian Elegy*, I don't claim Appalachian identity, but I do claim Appalachian solidarity – and by extension, a solidarity with all wild, natural regions.

Buried Creek has been one of those wild, natural regions on the losing end of development. Some would call this a small loss comparatively; others might consider it no loss at all given the families that lived and worked and gave to their communities from the homes created by development and served by the creek as a storm sewer. Rather than keeping the creek clean, though, we collectively use it to haul away our pollutants – motor oil, gasoline, transmission fluid, engine coolant, detergents, turpentine, anything that drips and drains from vehicles, buildings, streets, and parking lots. To keep the pipeline beneath our neighborhood free of trash and clogging, the water company installed a grate in front of the pipe leading to Buried Creek's underworld, and posted rebar several feet in front of the grate as another line of defense. Not long after Mike and I moved here, the city placed a chain-link fence where the creek enters our city and property from Elsmere as the first line of defense, but the pile of creek wrack grew so large behind it, the fence finally collapsed. "To a river, as to any natural force, an obstruction is merely an opportunity," writes Wendell Berry in *The Unforeseen Wilderness*. "If its way is obstructed then it goes around the obstruction or under it or over it and, flowing past it, wears it away." Buried Creek was, and remains, a natural water force during periods of heavy rain and melting snow.

Following the creek's occasional floodwaters, I have pulled from our bottomland all sorts of one-time treasures and obstructions. Some are merely predictable: soft drink and beer cans, bottles and wrappers, rusted metal, Styrofoam cups, all manner of plastic shrapnel, and a beaver's dam worth of wood. Some border on postmodern whimsy – doll heads, toy guns, basketballs, footballs, a Slinky, a Christmas wreath – while others take the prize for stereotype: old shoes, car tires, seat cushions, the bottom drawer from a white stove. A few are far too intimate – boxer shorts, condom wrappers, a tampon tube. Others are purely ironic: a red and white float from a fishing pole; the brush-end of a broom. Our family stands as guilty as anyone. In the aftermath of my father's long illness and death in 1972, his old metal roller was left in the back corner of the yard. For more than thirty years, it rusted into a hole-ridden hull the flooding creek could shove like a foundering ship. In deeper water it would have sunk out of sight; it now sits largely submerged in the creek bed, a family fossil. An opportunity, though not quite the one Berry had in mind, for the creek to wear away what it creates new passage around.

And yet, in spite of its unnatural filth and losses, Buried Creek at times still runs with surprises. I have seen asters, buttercups, garlic mustard, butterweed, wild blue violet, and white snakeroot bloom along its bank and bottom of our yard. Deer cut a path through these wildflowers, climbing the hill for a meal of our birdseed before continuing their journey along the water line. The creek still pools in the spring or after summer storms; robins, starlings, cardinals bathe in it and drink. A pair of mallard ducks visit for a few weeks each spring, swim and feed there (when they aren't eating our bird seed), and sit along its vine-covered, southern bank. The creek offers in miniature its river behaviors; it has gentle meanders, and deposits silt and gravel bars in the middle of its bed, re-shaping or moving them over time and the weather. In spring of 2014 I kept an eye on tadpoles, and later surprised a frog, sometimes off the bank into the water, and sometimes from the water to a mud hole under vines.

Then in late August that year, the air thick enough to build a house with, I arrived home from campus in the late afternoon amid the gradual clearing behind a thunderstorm. As the sun broke through thinning clouds and the tops of trees, it lit the west end of the creek and yard with slanting walls of light through baby rain and rising earth steam, everything green and golden. I walked to that end of the yard, but once I was in the wall of light the foliage let through, I could not see the light I was in. I was as "blind" to that light as I had been to the geography of my childhood: the valley carved by Buried Creek. Like any fog, what appeared distinct from a distance was more felt than seen when it surrounded me.

All of this unexpected beauty where Buried Creek muddies along as a storm sewer: its intersection of muck and clarity reminded me of the work that writers do. A river or flowing stream of any size is like a curious, imaginative mind. It takes in whatever comes. It may leave it behind, or carry it along, or slowly turn it into something else. A working stream isn't entirely independent; it needs gravity, gradient, and weather – a given amount of stability punctuated by change – to move through its larger course of existence, to be change itself. Its currents are a kind of handwriting. A river lives its research and is its story. It can teach us – it taught me – to keep looking.

Buried Creek had more secrets to reveal when I located

it on a U.S. Geological Survey map of the area. It is an intermittent stream – one that flows primarily when it rains rather than constantly – with headwaters near the Elsmere City Building on Garvey Avenue, one of the city's main thoroughfares. Concrete, brick, and asphalt have not stopped the way of water's underground insistence. More interesting is where it goes. Buried Creek flows into Rice Creek (another partially buried creek serving as a storm sewer route), which flows into Bullock Pen Creek, which flows into Banklick Creek, which flows into the Licking River. This is not surprising given that we live within the Licking River watershed, but I am captivated by the fact that my father purchased a property in 1960 – the last house and property of his life – that didn't just resemble, on a small scale, the farm he grew up on; it was physically, geographically tied to it. By way of water, he had returned in middle age to the farm he couldn't wait to leave as a young man. I don't know whether or not he was aware of the extent to which his life had come full-circle.

Granted, some would call this a tenuous connection at best. Banklick Creek enters the Licking north of Pendleton County, linking this property to the farm the way the Licking's headwaters in Magoffin County link my family to Appalachia: from a distance. And I would agree that this knowledge doesn't place me within the confines of a particular way of life (farming) or region (Appalachia). Instead it expands my sense of what it means to *be from*, of what and where I call home. Buried Creek helped me uncover this, its line of water and my lines of writing coursing toward new ground.

I now know that I have both genealogical and geographical lineages. My ancestors arrived and settled, some moved and settled again, or stayed in one place, but their locations extend geographically by the natural forces and landscape features they lived near – a creek, a river, a ridge – to areas they may not have known themselves. In the case of streams, that extension is simultaneously back to their headwaters, and forward to their tailwaters and larger cycle of life, again to places that my family members may never see, but to which they and others they don't know are connected geographically. Awareness of this can change *what is mine* into *ours*, and *what is theirs* into *mine also*, in a caretaking, rather than a grasping sense. Activists involved in various environmental causes put this awareness into practice, but individuals outside of those movements can gain this awareness on their own, as many have. "We all live downstream" is a popular slogan, but we all live upstream and *alongstream* as well. Is it necessary for me literally to be from Appalachia? No. Is it necessary for me to acknowledge my link to those mountains? Absolutely. At the very least this abstract connection with its roots in the physical world can spark imagination and compassion.

In several of the poems I drafted for the series described above, I incorporated language from property deeds, my father's textbooks, and newspaper clippings. Often these words or phrases resonate with a power that shakes my bones, as if they might reveal a secret I can't quite grasp but am trying to write to, that I carry in me somewhere the way my father carried the farm and its river. One of these phrases comes from his textbook, *Gano's Commercial Law* (1929), in the section that discusses real estate ownership and sales, and the boundaries or "monuments" used in deeds to identify properties legally. The phrase is: "A creek is a monument." In legal terms, this means a creek can officially mark the border of a property, and in doing so it simultaneously marks an end and a beginning of either property, as well as a point at which land and people align. In the geographical rather than legal sense, the creek as a monument also provides lineage to its deeper, richer points: source, destination, and return. In other words, the creek is a monument to the past, present, and future.

Rivers and creeks: over the long run they may be independent of us, but they are never isolated from their surroundings, and we are never independent of them. They have been places, they are going places, and yet when we visit their banks they stand before us, far more than their water, an entity of light and air that makes of motion a *place*. As I learned from Buried Creek, even the most "unspectacular streams" and ordinary places can reveal stories worth knowing if we make the effort to observe them on their terms. In both an imaginative and real sense, their terms become ours, and our sense of place, of home, becomes enlarged.

I turn to my dictionary now, where *monument* holds other meanings: something constructed and maintained to keep alive the memory of a person or event; a structure surviving from a former period; writing or other artistic work serving as a memorial; any work perceived to have lasting significance. An obsolete definition of *monument* is *tomb*. Buried Creek, my river, is all of these. From our house on Buried Creek, I remain connected to the Licking River, Appalachia, and the larger scope of their effects. This includes their losses and resilience, our tending and negligence. In Buried Creek runs my river autobiography. To borrow a phrase current in our digital age, I am "logged in" by its waters.

Acknowledgments

I thank Richard Hague, Pauletta Hansel, and Sherry Cook Stanforth for making possible the Community of Creative Writers Retreat at the education center of the Thomas More College Biology Field Station in Campbell County, Kentucky.

Jonathan Goolsby

apprenticeship

look here,
you see the ragged corners of that house?
those you must put into your work —
not just scalloped shake siding,
not just old, robin's-egg paint,
no

show me the copper pinnacle of the house.

see how it reflects
and is reflected in plate glass:
this is the poetry act embodied.

in your quiet time,
in your incantation time,
you must reflect and be reflected.

look here,
the way the sunset rounds the very corners of that house.
you'll notice an orange fuzziness at the edges:
train yourself to see not just outside but inside as well,
train yourself to see through its windows, around the drawn shades.

can you see the dimmer switches from here?
can you see to turn them on?

I say you can and you must.

the best poems will start at the roof-point,
lead me down through attic rafters
and disturb the bats,

they'll escort me through the upstairs, pause in the master's suite,
nose in the bathroom vanity and read medicine bottles
(only the interesting bottles, mind):
they'll take cotton balls from medicine bottles,
place cotton balls in provocative rows on the sink,
close the bathroom door softly,
leave just a crack.

look here,
the very best poems
do not breathe in the front parlor.

they empty ice trays in the kitchen,
put them back in the freezer without refilling.
it is not enough to inventory the silver:
tell of the scratches in the finish of a butter knife,
tell of their scandal.

the very best poems linger on the basement stairs
long enough to hear each downward creaking echo
and
upon reaching the sump-pump,
they turn that whole house on its pointed gables,
leave it balanced:
a safety razor stood on edge.

this is language, study.
this you must do, my study.

this is the task at hand:
a paint-flaking clapboard,
a rusty widow's watch.

William Scott Hanna

Directional

West, where
you came up
from the river
even more beautiful
than the orange red
of the dying day.

East, where
all children imagine
worlds beyond
their knowing
dawning.

Here, where
you cannot see
the river,
but you know
it is there, just beyond
the trees, footing the hills,

as sure as you know
a vein lies
under skin,

a voice waits
behind closed lips,

thousands
of invisible years
envelop the life of a stone
worn by that same river
you cannot see,

the sound
of the baby's cry lingers
between her silent sleeping
and the few still seconds
before her waking,

a seed-star
hides inside every apple
just as my mother showed me
when I was five,

and the water
in the river is
moving
was moving
will move
rock and stone
and dirt and mud
and love.

South, where
the universe expands
beyond our seeing
beyond our knowing
beyond
light and dust and dark.

North, where
your love is a window
locked against winter,
or an apple, unpicked,
your star, waiting.

Michael Henson

Trampoline: an Illustrated Novel by Robert Gipe

(Ohio University Press, 2015) 312 pages

I first met Robert Gipe at a reading during Seedtime on the Cumberland at the studios of WMMT. He read from *Trampoline* and totally blew the audience away with the humor and poignancy of what he read.

I remember thinking, this guy is a monster; this is the real thing.

So now, by way of Ohio University Press, the book is out. What on earth do you call a book like this?

A young adult novel with cussing and drugs?

A graphic novel with lots of extra words between panels.

The author calls it an "illustrated novel."

I call it a damn fine piece of writing. This is a first novel for Gipe who is known for several other things, including illustrator, educator, actor, and storyteller. His drawings for t-shirts and journals have decorated many a chest and many a page. He is also noted as the director at the Cumberland Community College in Harlan County, Kentucky. Now he can add novelist, or even better, innovative novelist to his credits.

In this book, Gipe creates a character, the teenage Dawn Jewell, who is as moody and conflicted as a girl can be. Like many a young Appalachian person in this age of sad addiction, she lives with her grandmother, Cora, who has taken on the task of raising awareness of the evils of mountaintop removal. Early in the novel, she takes Dawn with her to a public hearing, where Dawn discovers her voice as a spokesperson.

Problem is, this stance is not popular with a whole web of people, including family and friends, with the result that, already angry and conflicted over the death of her father in the mines and her mother's subsequent spiral into addiction, Dawn lashes out in all directions and she encounters disaster and near-disaster with a frequency not seen since the Perils of Pauline.

Spoiler alert: Dawn survives, prospers, and even finds true love, though not as she had hoped or expected. But that's how things go.

Frequent peril can take a book perilously close to melodrama or farce. But Gipe rescues his heroine and her book through an utterly wicked sense of humor and his pitch-perfect ear for dialogue. Dawn can deliver rich one-liners. But the real treasures are in extended scenes like the one in which Dawn's mother and her mother's friend Big Jan decide to dye Dawn's hair green. The passage is too subtle to capture a sense of it from a short quote; suffice it to say that it has the sense of real people talking.

It's easy to get self-righteous about mountaintop removal. It's a genuine, clear-cut evil. The people who conduct it have to construct passionate and elaborate rationalizations to justify it and to continue it. But they are human beings, with all the fears and strengths of human beings. One among the several strengths of Gipe's book is that he allows individuals on all sides of this issue their full humanity. No one is a plaster saint; no one is condemned.

This is a book which will live; it is important now; it will continue to be important for many years to come.

Jonathan Goolsby

An Undeniable, Unmistakable *World*: Reviewing Michael Henson's *The Way the World Is: The Maggie Boylan Stories*

Maggie Boylan is an addict. She's a liar. And she's a thief.

She's desperate. Trapped. Unlucky.

And she's strong. Protective. Kind.

Maggie Boylan is all those things. And the stories she figures into — the stories that describe Henson's rusted-out *Winesburg* — show us that rural Ohio, in the grip of economic collapse and neglect, is a complicated place.

Sherwood Anderson's famous cycle is certainly a spiritual antecessor to Henson's, in that both explore the interconnectedness, unspoken and sometimes unspeakable secrets of a small town in the shadow of Appalachia.

Anderson's bright-eyed cubby George Willard works at the town newspaper, which exists for its one and only expressed goal "to mention by name in each issue, as many inhabitants as possible of the inhabitants of the village" (134).

People in Winesburg want their stories told, as Christopher Sergel wrote into his 1960 dramatization of the cycle, "so the terrible isolation of their lives can break" (82).

But they are careful to use George Willard as the means of curating their stories, of presenting them in the most positive light and deflecting attention from their indiscretions. Compare this with the people in Henson's Wolf Creek, who in many cases only tell the sides of their stories that portray them favorably.

Does a deputy steal money from Maggie because he is corrupt, or because he wants to keep her from shooting it up her arm? Does the judge who threatens to throw Maggie under the jail should she break post-rehab probation really care about saving her from herself, or does he need a whipping girl to deflect public inquiry into his own doings and thus keep his elected seat on the county bench?

Winesburg and Wolf Creek both admirably portray the phenomenon that we now see played out so conspicuously on social media, but which in reality has always existed:

Politicking. Peacocking. Pancaking and preening.

People want us to believe they are who they say they are.

George Willard tells what he knows because it his job and, in doing his job, he hopes to escape his hometown.

Maggie Boylan tells what she knows because she wants to escape, too — to escape her well-earned reputation. To win back her jailed husband. To fade finally into the background of the town, to stop people's tongues wagging about *her*.

The problem for both, of course, is that rural (sub, "Appalachian," if you will) Ohio has a tendency to trap people. It always has.

At the turn of the last century, the people of Winesburg were bound to their hardscrabble farms, to their shabby small town businesses, to their diminishing trade with countrymen whose attention was fixated evermore west of rural Ohio.

The people of Winesburg were wrestling with the inevitable trough that came after the crest of Manifest Destiny had long passed them by — and many turned to various forms of vice to forget in the short-term, ignoring that they would receive from their vices only more misery in the long-run.

Funny how things change, but don't change.

For the people in Henson's Wolf Creek are bound to their defaulting mortgages, to their shabby small town businesses, to the last gasps of Big Coal, industrialization and the Great Briar Migration. To forget their misery, many of the people in Wolf Creek turn either to abusing or trafficking: illicit pot, opioid pain medications, heroin.

But there's an important point of contrast: In *Wines-*

burg, George Willard is finally able to escape when he gives up everything and purchases a train ticket to somewhere.

Maggie Boylan has no such luxury. She has a home with no power, a truck that won't start and a PO watching over her shoulder. There's only zen-like acceptance that this is the way the world is, or there is more to grind on her soul, as Henson depicted on pages 130-131:

> Oh my God, she thought, what the fuck am I doing?
>
> She put her hands to her temples and turned back to the house. She stumbled to the couch and collapsed.
>
> Shivering, nauseous, utterly emptied of thought, bereft of either hope or despair, she curled up into herself like a child.
>
> "Oh my God," she whispered.
>
> As if it were a prayer.

George Willard could take a train and look forward to the future. Maggie Boylan can only look around and accept the things she cannot change.

Of *Winesburg*, in the *New York Times Book Review*, William Lyon Phelps wrote that Anderson's "characters are actuated by motives not exterior; their actions give something of the startling effect of a head and shoulders snapping suddenly out of a hidden trapdoor in an empty room" (353).

Henson's characters are no less admirably crafted. In Wolf Creek, no one is entirely guiltless, nor entirely guilty. Motivations are as milky and murky as an oxycodone tablet crushed, mixed and cold shot.

But, even in this dale of people dazed, there are brilliant moments of clarity. Of compassion. Of deep pathos. At times, of humor, even.

Henson has, in his Maggie Boylan stories, a book of as surely uncommon merit as HL Mencken reportedly thought

Winesburg (White, note 11).

It's fitting that this review is written with memory of the 1990s' Cornbread Mafia trials, in a region still gasping for air in the toxic sludge left by 2008's economic dam burst, during a news cycle that has relentlessly probed the 2016 massacre of a Pike County family.

For, like Maggie Boylan, we seem to be caught up in a socioeconomic Charybdis. And we seem resigned to it.

Henson shares with us his penetrating insight into this world. Here is a master of narrative and of place. Here he presents us with a town full of people that we, living in the oft-hazy shadow of Appalachia, *know*.

Works Cited

Anderson, Sherwood. *Winesburg, Ohio* [Norton Critical Edition]. New York: W.W. Norton & Co., 1996. Print.

Henson, Michael. *The Way the World Is: The Maggie Boylan Stories*. Omaha: Brighthorse Books, 2015.

Phelps, William Lyon. *The New York Times Book Review* 29 June 1919: 353. Print.

Sergel, Christopher. *Sherwood Anderson's Winesburg, Ohio: A Dramatization*. Woodstock, Ill.: The Dramatic Publishing Company, 1960: 82. Digital text.

White, Ray Lewis. "Mencken's Lost Review of *Winesburg, Ohio*." *Notes on Modern American*

Chuck Stringer

New Books by Three Appalachian Poets

Sherry Cook Stanforth: *Drone String* (Bottom Dog Press, 2015)

Like the creek water flowing through the book's initial poem, "Woman, Creek Walking," so flows the rich heritage of Appalachian voices, stories, music, and places through Sherry Cook Stanforth's first collection of poems. In *Drone String* we hear "the tones/of four generations steered straight/by aunts and grandmothers," and witness the creation of a feminine self and voice as strong and original as "those stone hard ballads" singing from her mother's dulcimer. These are *traditional* poems in the root meaning of that word, poems *to hand over, deliver, entrust,* and we the readers should be grateful that this gifted poet has chosen "to carry, then/pass on such gifts with care" ("Barlow Knife"). "*Tall,* they used to whisper/in her ear. She carries tall/ inside her heart" ("This Time"); and if you read only one poem, don't miss her stunning performance piece, "App, Too," to experience the full extent of what a *tall* Appalachian woman has to say.

Pauletta Hansel: *Tangle* (Dos Madres Press, 2015)

In this her fifth and latest collection of poems, Appalachian poet and teacher (and now the first Poet Laureate of Cincinnati) Pauletta Hansel shows us how the practice of poetry—work of both the day ("attention with eye and ear/and pen") and the night ("to let what rises/swim in sleep's deep dark")—can take us deeper than our fears, our sorrows, our longings, our regrets; how the disciple of this craft and art, when practiced with this poet's honesty, humility, and ability, can fill us again and again with grace and gratitude, knowledge and illumination, wonder and delight. In five sections, the poet takes us on a journey through the tangle of past and present selves (and *personae*) as they move through the corresponding tangle of events and relationships that is her life. Reading these poems, we come away refreshed, enriched, "replenished." What this reader marvels at and admires so much is the powerful intensity of Hansel's voice—ever attentive, intelligent, insightful, yet when it needs to be, quietly defiant.

Richard Hague: *Where Drunk Men Go: A Long Poem* (Dos Madres Press, 2015)

Taking Rilke's advice to young poets to "live the questions now," prolific author and teacher Richard Hague, in this long performance poem, lives into the question of *Where Drunk Men Go*. First published in *Appalachian Journal*, and later as a section in the award-winning *Alive in Hard Country* (Bottom Dog Press, 2003), this revised and updated version includes a new Prologue by fellow author/musician and fifty-year friend Michael Henson, who also provides instrumental and vocal accompaniment in the poem's performance (performed recently at Thomas More College, where Hague is the current Writer-in-Residence). Hague's question takes him, like a modern-day Odysseus, on a long journey into the fallen world of a drunk, who has "No choice but cry out, curse, complain" against the gods and himself and his condition, which we come to see as our own very human condition.

CONTRIBUTORS

Izzy Broomfield was born at Mary Breckenridge and grew up in Berea and didn't start writing until out of the region and missing it. Izzy says, "I write about here, about not here, and about the distance between the two in today's world."

Joyce Compton Brown earned degrees from Appalachian State University and from the University of Southern Mississippi. She studied poetry at Hindman (Appalachian Writers Workshop) and at Berea College workshops. She taught at Gardner-Webb University and has published in numerous journals. Her chapbook *Bequest* is being published by Finishing Line Press.

Arwen Careaga is from Martin County, Kentucky. She presently resides in Lexington with her family, reading when she can and writing when she can't help it. She is no longer under 30.

Richard Childers is a Kentuckian from Estill County. He is a graduate of Berea College with a degree in English. His short story, "Hocked" was chosen as the runner-up for the 2015 Gurney Norman Prize for Fiction and will be published in *The Limestone Journal* this spring.

Leslie Clark holds an MFA from the Bennington Writing Seminars in Vermont. Her poems have been published in *Four Corners, Art Spike*, and *The Bennington Review*, as well as online. She was born in Fairmont, West Virginia, and moved with her mother to Cincinnati at age 7, spending summers and holiday vacations with relatives in Fairmont.

Omope Carter Daboiku is an internationally acclaimed storyteller and emergent writer. She directs poetry programs for the Paul Laurence Dunbar house in Dayton, Ohio. Her poem is dedicated to her descendants – Adesola and Tinuade, both of whom are under 30, educated, politically active, gainfully employed and proud of their Appalachian heritage.

Willie Davis's fiction has appeared in *The Kenyon Review, the Berkeley Fiction Review, Salon.com,* and *The Guardian*, among others, and is winner of the Willesden Herald International Short Story Prize and the Katherine Anne Porter Prize and is a fellow of the Kentucky Arts Council.

Angelyn DeBord's art rises up from the beautiful mountain land where she was born and raised. She has a degree in Visual Art and has studied painting in France, Italy and Germany. DeBord has exhibited throughout the Appalachian Mountains. Her shrines, altars and paintings are in many collections throughout American and as far away as Australia.

Cody S. Decker is from Wayne County, Kentucky, and currently lives in Lexington, Kentucky. He began writing six years ago when he was twenty years old and has been living the way of the written word ever since. He enjoys a nice cold glass of bourbon but won't say no if it's room temperature.

Nancy Dillingham is a sixth-generation Dillingham from Big Ivy in western North Carolina. She is author of nine books of poetry and short fiction and is co-editor of four anthologies of western North Carolina women writers.

Wendy Dinwiddie is an MFA candidate at the University of Alabama. Her writing has appeared in *2nd and Church, Kudzu,* and *The Red Mud Review.*

Cecile Dixon holds an MFA from Bluegrass Writers Studio. Her work has appeared in *The Dead Mule School of Southern Literature* and other journals.

Hilda Downer has been a long-time member of the Southern Appalachian Writers Cooperative. Her first book of poetry, *Bandana Creek*, depicts her experiences growing up. *Sky Under the Roof*, published by Bottom Dog Press, was a Nautilus Golden winner for poetry in 2014. She has been nominated twice for a Pulitzer Prize.

Ashleigh Gill is an MFA student in Children's Literature at Hollins University, but grew up in Hinton, West Virginia. She received her BA in English Literature and BS in Education from Concord University. Gill is playwright and co-founder of the Hinton theatre company, Ars Creo. She lives in Roanoke, Virginia.

Kris Gillis teaches high school English and lives in Bellevue, Kentucky, with his dog, PJ, and his cat, Miranda. His poetry has appeared in the literary journals *Words* and *The White Squirrel.*

Jonathan Goolsby was raised in Clermont County, Ohio, on Appalachia's westernmost frontier — a McCoy great-grandson and fourth-great-grandnephew of Jenny Wylie. His work has appeared in *Pine Mountain Sand & Gravel - Vol. 18, Limestone* and *Midwestern Gothic*. He believes he owes the Cincinnati Writers Project and the Southern Appalachian Writers Cooperative many thanks.

William Graham, resident of Boone, North Carolina, spends half of his time as an employee of a local homeless shelter and the other half doing the things he likes best. If you're looking for William, you will likely find him where there is good coffee, a tasty drink, and old friends.

Connie Jordan Green lives on an East Tennessee farm. She writes a newspaper column, poetry, and novels for young people. Her chapbooks, *Slow Children Playing* and *Regret Comes to Tea,* are from Finishing Line Press, and a full-length collection, *Household Inventory*, won the Brick Road Poetry Press Award.

Richard Hague is a native of Steubenville, Ohio. His fifteen collections include *During the Recent Extinctions: New and Selected Poems 1984-2012,* which won the Weatherford Award for poetry and *Alive in Hard Country* which was named 2003 Poetry Book of the Year by the Appalachian Writers Association.

Scott Hanna is a life-long resident of the upper Ohio Valley. He received degrees from West Liberty State College, Marshall University, and Indiana University of Pennsylvania. He currently teaches at West Liberty University.

Pauletta Hansel, managing editor of this journal, is honored to have her work included alongside these young Appalachian writers, having once been one herself. She is the author of five poetry collections, including *Tangle*, in which "Girl Villanelle" first appeared. She is the first Poet Laureate of Cincinnati, Ohio.

Melissa Helton is an Associate Professor of English at Southeast Kentucky Community and Technical College. Her work has appeared in *Pikeville Review, Kudzu, The Notebook, Still: the Journal*, and more. Her first chapbook, *Inertia: a Study,* is available through Finishing Line Press. She lives and writes in the Appalachians of Kentucky.

Michael Henson is a co-editor of this magazine. His collection, *The Way the World Is: the Maggie Boylan Stories*, won the 2014 Brighthorse Prize in Short Fiction. His most recent work is *A Small Room with Trouble on My Mind and Other Stories.*

Thomas Alan Holmes teaches at East Tennessee State University. His work has appeared in *Louisiana Literature, Valparaiso Poetry Review, Appalachian Heritage, North American Review, and Still: the Journal.* Other poems are forthcoming in *Zone 3* and *The World Is Charged: Poetic Engagements with Gerard Manley Hopkins* from Clemson University Press.

Dory L. Hudspeth is an herbalist, freelance writer, and poet living in Alvaton, Kentucky. Her poems have appeared in *Rattle, Wavelength, Shenandoah, Sow's Ear Review, Slant, Runes, Atlanta Review,* and other journals. Her first poetry collection is *Enduring Wonders* from WordTech Press and her chapbook is *I'll Fly Away* from Finishing Line Press.

Donna Isaac (*donnaisaacpoet.com*) grew up in the Appalachian region of Virginia, North Carolina, and Tennessee and now lives in Minnesota where she teaches writing and literature. She has two poetry chapbooks: *Tommy from Red Dragonfly* Press and *Holy Comforter* from Red Bird Chapbooks. Her work has appeared in *White Stag,* the *St. Paul Almanac* and other journals.

Andrew Jensen is a student at Thomas More College. He has lived his whole life in Campbell County, Kentucky. His favorite place to be is outdoors in the woods. He is a member of two local musical groups, playing the banjo and the mountain dulcimer, as well as singing.

Joshua Jones just finished his MFA in poetry at the University of Massachusetts Boston and just began his PhD at the University of North Texas. His poems have appeared in *The Broad River Review, Sow's Ear Poetry Review,* and *Kindred.*

Sabrina Jones is a native of Logan County, West Virginia, and a current English instructor at Marshall University. She is passionate about both reading and writing – particularly in the fields of young adult and Appalachian literature. Her creative work has been published in *The Anthology of Appalachian Writers* and *Not Taking a Fence.*

Sandi Keaton-Wilson of Somerset, Kentucky, has had her prose, poetry, and plays published in journals and anthologies including *Appalachian Heritage, Appalachian Journal, Coal: an Anthology* and *Now & Then. Boundaries,* her play on mountaintop removal, has been staged in Berea, Somerset, and at the Manhattan Studio Club.

Clyde Kessler of Radford, Virginia, is a founding member of the Blue Ridge Discovery Center, an environmental education organization with programs in Virginia and North Carolina. He is also a regional editor for *Virginia Birds*, a publication of the Virginia Society of Ornithology.

Steven Paul Lansky taught at Miami University of Ohio. He has published in *The Brooklyn Rail, Cosmonauts Avenue, Black Clock 20, Whole Terrain, New Flash Fiction Review,* and *Article 25*. His audionovel *Jack Acid* is available from cdbaby.com. He graduated from The University of Tampa's Low-Residency MFA in 2015.

Cathy Cultice Lentes is a frequent contributor to Appalachian publications including *Pine Mountain Sand & Gravel, Appalachian Heritage*, and anthologies such as *Every River on Earth: Writing From Appalachian Ohio* (Ohio University Press, 2015). She is the author of the poetry chapbook, *Getting the Mail* (Finishing Line Press, 2016). Visit her at www.cathyculticelentes.com.

Rebecca S. Lindsay, editor of *Pegasus*, the poetry journal of the Kentucky State Poetry Society, has had poetry published in *Pegasus, For a Better World,* and *Change Happens.* Two poems placed first in the Green River Grande Poetry Award, "Shenandoah Refugees: October 1864" (2009) and "The Baker of Pompeii" (2014).

Lyn May is a previously unpublished writer pursuing her BA in creative writing at Warren Wilson College. She has had the pleasure of studying under writers Catherine Reid and Rachel Himmelheber. May's family is rooted in Mingo County, West Virginia, where she remembers much of her childhood.

Juanita Mays is a native of Scioto County, Ohio, but now resides in Milford. She has won numerous awards and has been published in a number of literary journals. Her poems "The Coolest" and "Phyllis and the Wind" won first place awards for the Kentucky State Poetry Society.

Amy McCleese grew up in Flemingsburg, Kentucky, and remains invested in the places and experiences of her home region. Her poetry explores the interplay of the sacred and the everyday in these settings. She is a doctoral student in Rhetoric and Composition and the 2016 recipient of the University of Louisville Creative Writing Award for Poetry.

Christopher McCurry is an editor at Accents Publishing and a high school English teacher. His poems are published in several journals, including *Diode, Louisville Review, Rabbit Catastrophe Review,* the *LA Review, Rattle* and others. His chapbook *Nearly Perfect* is available from Two of Cups Press. He is co-founder of Workhorse, a collective for writers.

Michaela Miller is a native of Barbourville, Kentucky. She is a student at Western Kentucky University where she is majoring in Photojournalism with a minor in Creative Writing. Michaela fell in love with poetry in her sophomore fall semester at WKU when she took an Intro to Creative Writing Class from

Mary Ellen Miller.

Aaron Morris is a student in the MFA program at West Virginia Wesleyan College. His work has appeared in *ABZ, Et Cetera, Jet Fuel Review, Kanawha Review,* and *Turtleshell.* He teaches writing and literature as an adjunct at West Virginia State University.

Carrie Mullins' novel *Night Garden* was published by Old Cove Press in 2016. She has had fiction published in *Chicago Quarterly Review, Appalachian Heritage, Kudzu,* the online journal *Still,* and *Appalachia Now: Short Stories of Contemporary Appalachia.* Mullins grew up in Mt. Vernon, Kentucky, where she still lives.

Maggie Naas lives in Wise, Virginia, and is mother to two beautiful girls. She plans to graduate from the University of Virginia-Wise with a degree in sociology.

Jeremy Paden, an Affrilachian Poet, teaches Spanish at Transylvania University and has authored three chapbooks: *Broken Tulips* (Accents Press, 2013), *ruina montium* (Broadstone Press, 2016), and *Delicate Matters* (Argus House Books, 2016). His poems have appeared in various and sundry places, like *Beloit Poetry Journal, Hampden-Sydney Review, Louisville Review, Still.*

Linda Parsons is an editor at the University of Tennessee in Knoxville whose work has appeared in *The Georgia Review, Iowa Review, Prairie Schooner,* and others. Her fourth collection, *This Shaky Earth*, was published by Texas Review Press and her plays *Macbeth is the New Black* and *Under the Esso Moon* have both been recently been performed.

Matthew Parsons, a native of southern West Virginia, was raised on a farm by a librarian and a bluegrass musician. He received a BA in Appalachian Studies from Berea College and has been known to speak his mind. He now lives in a little hut in Olive Hill, Kentucky.

Rhonda Pettit is the author of the poetic drama, *The Global Lovers*; the chapbook, *Fetal Waters*; and a series of collages, and collaborative poems and triptychs with H. Michael Sanders, as part of the *Gaps and Overlaps* exhibition at the UC Blue Ash Art Gallery. She is professor of English at UC Blue Ash College.

Christopher Petruccelli is trying to survive his first winter in Fairbanks, Alaska. His poetry has appeared or is forthcoming in *Appalachian Heritage, Cider Press Review, Rappahannock Review, Still: The Journal* and elsewhere. His chapbook, *Action at a Distance*, is available from UIndy's Etchings Press.

Matt Prater, from Saltville, Virginia, is winner of both the George Scarbrough Prize for Poetry and the James Still Prize for Short Story. His work has appeared in *Appalachian Journal, The Honest Ulsterman, The Moth,* and in *Still: the Journal.* He is an MFA candidate at Virginia Tech.

Dale Marie Prenatt is a poet and storyteller from Buffalo Creek, West Virginia, by way of Eastern Kentucky. Her work has been featured in *Inscape Literary Magazine, Appalachian Women's Journal,* and in this magazine and on National Public Radio. She lives in Lexington, Kentucky.

Nicole Rahe is a native of Clermont County, Ohio, and has lived on the edge of country and city her entire life. She writes poetry in the time between raising three young children with her husband of 16 years. She is also a member of the Greater Cincinnati Writer's League.

Shawna Kay Rodenberg is the founder and host of Slant, a monthly poetry reading in Evansville Indiana and teaches at a community college in Eastern Kentucky. Her work has appeared in *New Millenium Writings, Structo, drafthorse, Free State Review, Crab Creek Review, Kudzu*, and others. She lives on a dairy goat farm in southern Indiana.

Amanda Rodriguez is an environmental activist living in Weaverville, North Carolina. She holds a BA from Antioch College and an MFA from Queens University in Charlotte. She writes and edits for *Bitch Flicks*. Her short story "The Woman Who Fell in Love with a Mermaid" was published in *Germ Magazine.*

Roberta Schultz is a singer-songwriter originally from Grant's Lick, Kentucky. Her poems and lyrics have appeared in *Slant, Motif, Waypoints, Kudzu, The Notebook*, and other publications. Her chapbook, *Outposts on the Border of Longing*, was published by Finishing Line Press.

Mindy Dawn Silvergarden lives in the mountains of Centre County, Pennsylvania, where she enjoys the great outdoors while taking the leisurely route to a degree in Economics and Labor Studies.

Misty Skaggs, 34, currently resides at the very far end of Beartown Ridge Road in Elliott County, Kentucky. Her work has been published in *Still, New Madrid, Limestone, Inscape, The Pikeville Review,* and *Kudzu* as well as many other literary journals. Skaggs' writing deals almost exclusively with the culture and people of the East Kentucky foothills.

Kelsey A. Solomon recently received her MA in English from East Tennessee State University with emphases in Appalachian, modern/postmodern British, and early American literature. She will serve as an adjunct instructor of English for ETSU and other neighboring community colleges around the Johnson City area. She was raised in Hamblen County, Tennessee.

Aubrey Stanforth is a home-schooled eighth-grader involved in creative writing and music. She sings and plays guitar in a 3-generation Appalachian family band, Tellico. She is interested in astronomy, photography and theater, and enjoys exploring woods and creeks with her three siblings, parents and dogs. She takes Mandarin lessons and studies Spanish at Thomas More College.

Sherry Cook Stanforth is the founder/director of Thomas More College's Creative Writing Vision Program. She teaches fiction, poetry, environmental and ethnic literatures and serves as co-editor for *PMS&G*. Her poetry collection *Drone String* (Bottom Dog Press, 2015) is inspired by generational home places and her family's Appalachian music and storytelling tradition.

Daniel Stephenson would have been raised by wolves if there were any still alive. Instead, coyotes taught Daniel to lie, horned owls to question, and the neighborhood dogs to lead one astray. His soul was lost early in the Smokey Mountains, off some cliff etched by acid rain. He was baptized in the Clinch, drowned by DOE and dammed forever.

Chuck Stringer grew up on the Clinch and Tennessee rivers near Kingston, Tennessee, and belongs to the group of regional poets in the Thomas More College Creative Writing Vision Program. His work has been published in *Pine Mountain Sand & Gravel, The Licking River Review,* and *Words 2015*. He lives with wife Susan and cat Bella in Union, Kentucky.

Charles A. Swanson teaches in a new Academy for Engineering and Technology in the Southside region of Virginia where he also pastors a small church. He has two books of poems, *After the Garden* (MotesBooks) and *Farm Life and Legend* (Finishing Line Press.) His poem in this journal was written while still in high school.

Susan O'Dell Underwood directs the Creative Writing Program at Carson-Newman University, where she also teaches Appalachian lit courses. Besides two chapbooks, her work has appeared in a variety of journals and anthologies, including *Oxford American* and *The Southern Poetry Anthology: Tennessee.* She's a regular poetry reader on *Tennessee Shines,* a live radio program broadcast by WDVX in Knoxville.

Alicia Wright was born and raised in West Virginia and is an MFA candidate at Bowling Green State University in Ohio. Her work has appeared in *Bitterzoet, Kenning, Kestrel,* and several others. She is currently an assistant editor for *Mid-American Review.*

SUBMISSION GUIDELINES
Volume 20:
Appalachia: Stay or Go?

Deadline: April 15, 2017
Publication Date: October 2017

Volume 20 will use the theme of *Appalachia: Stay or Go*? This theme was recommended to us by Southern Appalachian Writers Cooperative writers watching their friends, neighbors and family members struggle with this question. Many writers within our community were once part of the Great Migration from Appalachia in the mid-twentieth century and have written (or may choose now to write) about their own or their family's choice to leave the region. Others are facing similar decisions now. And since we'll be presenting Volume 20 at the 2018 Appalachian Studies Conference in Cincinnati, with its theme of "Re-stitching the Seams: Appalachia Beyond Its Borders," the subject seems especially apt. But as always, we at *Pine Mountain Sand & Gravel* like to take a fairly broad approach to our themes—what else might be the subject of a "stay or go" decision? (Jobs, relationships, parties, churches, social groups, schools….) Unpublished work is preferred, but we aren't sticklers. Send us your best writing exploring *Appalachia: Stay or Go?*

What to send:
WRITERS

- Attach **one** text document per genre, Word preferred. This document should include cover letter, 50 word third person bio, all contact information (name, address, phone, email address), a list of titles and your poetry or prose submission. Please put all of this in the text document, even if some of the info is in your email.)

- **Poetry submissions**: up to 5 poems in one document please, no more than 10 pages.
- **Prose submission:** One piece of up to 5,000 words; shorter pieces (3,000 words or less) stand a better chance of publication. We will consider stories, essays, one-acts, memoir and book reviews. We love book reviews and will love you for sending one to us.
- **Submissions in more than one genre:** Attach one document for each genre, following the guidelines, and include your bio, contact info and cover letter in each.
- Your attached document should be named with your name (preferably last name first) and whether the submission is poetry or prose (e.g., Still, James poetry) which will match our filing system.
- Times New Roman, 12 point, single spaced for both poetry and prose, please. If you indent the first line of each new prose paragraph (rather than double spacing between) this, too, saves us time.
- Please make sure your name as you wish to see it in print is associated with each piece you send (under or above each title, for example).

VISUAL ARTISTS

- Send any 2D art, including black and white drawings, photos, comics, etc., that can be scaled effectively to a digest-sized page.
- We are also on the lookout for one color visual art piece for the cover, either as a wraparound cover (front and back) or front cover only.
- Send art in appropriate format, and cover letter, 50 word third person bio, all contact information (name, address, phone, email address), a list of titles in **one** text file.

Send via email to pmsg.journal@gmail.com, or contact us for an alternative form of submission.

Deadline: April 15, 2017 (Response in July 2017)

PLEASE, PLEASE, PLEASE follow these guidelines. Work pasted directly into the email message or sent as PDF attachment, or in other fonts or formatting is time-consuming to reformat and makes us cranky, as does opening up a bunch of documents from the same person, or having to trace unlabeled pieces back to their author's email. And you don't want cranky editors, now do you?